"Surrender and obedience are not popular themes in our culture which esteems autonomy and freedom. James A. Krisher demonstrates well that our humanness and salvation depend upon our saying yes to God. He challenges us to surrender to our creaturehood, to suffering and joy, to prayer and death. This book is to be prayed over as much as it is to be read."

† Robert F. Morneau
Auxiliary Bishop of Green Bay

"In a world that views surrender as weakness, Jim Krisher has provided a much-needed scriptural perspective on spiritual surrender. In this readable and profound book, Krisher guides the reader in discovering those ways in which surrender leads them to find God in the everyday events of their lives. Krisher illustrates through Scripture, the sharing of his experiences as a spiritual director, and his suggestions for prayer, that although surrender does not come easy, it does bring new life as people surrender themselves into the arms of a loving God."

Virginia Berglund Smith
McCormick Theological Seminary
Chicago, IL

"In his book, *Spiritual Surrender,* James Krisher has dared to write about a topic some would consider (at worst) unattractive or (at best) ambiguous. But Krisher shows with amazing clarity, spiritual surrender is not only a source of great peace and joy, it is also the fundamental movement of our life of faith. Although I enjoyed all the chapters, I thought the ones on 'Surrender in Pleasure and Joy' and 'The Final Surrender' (Death) were worth the price of the entire book! I also appreciated the various prayer exercises, for they helped me relate each chapter to my own lived experience."

Melannie Svoboda, S.N.D.
Author, *Traits of a Healthy Spirituality*

"The author describes 'surrender' as something that goes far beyond simple capitulation. His is not a 'laissez-faire' spirituality. Rather, surrender is a deliberately chosen attitude-cum-action that enables us to put ourselves and all that is ours in the hands of God. In clear, well-written chapters. Krisher tells us how to surrender not only in our sufferings, but also in our joys and pleasures (sometimes difficult to do), and even in our prayer life."

Norman J. Muckerman, C.SS.R.
Former editor, *Liguorian Magazine*

"Krisher's deft analysis of the need for 'spiritual surrender' as the key to deepening one's experience of God could replace a whole shelf of self-improvement books. He recognizes the skepticism that readers from our culture of self-assertion and victimization would bring to the topic. Krisher consistently reminds his readers that God is 'lover' not 'warrior'...and that distinction makes all the difference."

Professor Pheme Perkins
Boston College

"James Krisher has taken on a very difficult and important topic and handled it in a way I believe will be helpful to many people. It is the question of our resistance or subtle control in our relationship with God. We are often unaware of a deep seated reluctance to yield ourselves in any relationship.

"Krisher's examples and gentle readable style do not force or belittle the reader or the problem. Our experience of surrendering to pleasure is a wonderful antidote to the negative notions we have about surrender. A variety of prayer exercises are presented that may be helpful in themselves or as invitation to develop our own. Certainly there is no better way to move an insight from page to practice than by prayer. We have no greater teacher in the true meaning and practice of surrender than the One we meet in prayer."

Fr. Martin Boler, O.S.B.
Prior of Mt. Saviour Monastery
Pine City, NY

SPIRITUAL
Surrender

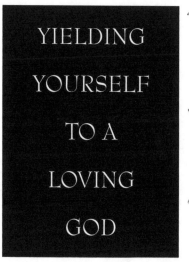

YIELDING

YOURSELF

TO A

LOVING

GOD

James A. Krisher

To Mary Ellen, beloved of God. For the joy you spread as light, I thank you. In Christ, Jim

TWENTY-THIRD PUBLICATIONS

Mystic, CT 06355

DEDICATION

To Debra,

with love and gratitude

The quotations of the Bible used in this book are from the *New Revised Standard Version* (©1989 Division of Christian Education of the National Council of Churches of Christ in the United States of America) and are reprinted with permission.

Twenty-Third Publications
185 Willow Street
P.O. Box 180
Mystic, CT 06355
(860) 536-2611
800-321-0411

ISBN 0-89622-721-9
Library of Congress Catalog Card Number 96-61816
Printed in the U.S.A.

Acknowledgments

I am grateful to the men and women who have permitted me to share bits of their stories with you in these pages. I am grateful, too, for the comments and encouragement offered by Carlyn Hachey, Marise May, O.S.F., and Vincent Elacqua. Their willingness to read and respond to my manuscript as the individual chapters unfolded was of great help to me. The practical advice offered by my former teacher, now friend, Dr. Pheme Perkins, has been invaluable. I have also appreciated the kindness shown to me by Neil Kluepfel, publisher at Twenty-Third Publications, and all his staff. It has been a pleasure to work with them.

Would that I could name all those who have encouraged me in this project, and indeed, throughout my years in ministry! I have been formed, affirmed, and supported by my parents, family, and friends, teachers and spiritual directors. Each has revealed to me something of "the depth of the riches and wisdom and knowledge of God" (Rom 11:33). I thank God especially for all that I've been given in my four children—Joe, Ben, Elizabeth, and young James—and for the precious gift of my wife Debra.

CONTENTS

INTRODUCTION   1

CHAPTER 1
THE MEANING OF SURRENDER   5

CHAPTER 2
ACCEPTING OUR CREATUREHOOD   13

CHAPTER 3
SURRENDER IN SUFFERING   25

CHAPTER 4
SURRENDER IN PLEASURE AND JOY   38

CHAPTER 5
SURRENDER IN PRAYER   51

CHAPTER 6
RESISTANCE TO SURRENDER   64

CHAPTER 7
THE FINAL SURRENDER   78

FOR FURTHER READING   87

INTRODUCTION

He was sitting opposite me on a padded rocker in the Merton Room of Stella Maris retreat house. We were in the fourth day of an eight-day directed retreat for clergy, and I had the privilege of serving as his director. Although outside the sun was shining bright, there was a tangible heaviness in the room as this man struggled to tell the story of a most burdensome situation in his life, and the frustration he felt at being unable to change it.

I felt frustrated, too. It's not easy to be admitted to another's pain only to recognize that you have no solutions, no answers to the questions, no healing balm for the bleeding wound. The familiar feelings of inadequacy were rising within me, and recognizing this, I silently asked for divine assistance.

In doing so, I glanced through the window to the expanse of blue sky. Now, perhaps I've watched *The Wizard of Oz* one time too many, but for an instant my mind's eye saw a word as clearly as if it had been written in giant letters of smoke across the firmament: SURRENDER. It was a word of grace, one we both needed to hear as we sat in that little room.

At once I felt myself relaxing, trusting anew the call that God had given me, and remembering for the millionth time that it wasn't my job to have solutions. I may have even smiled as I spoke that one word to him: "Surrender." Upon hearing this, the man shifted in his chair and we both were silent for a moment as God's invitation penetrated our hearts.

From that point on, the heaviness lifted. When he left the retreat at week's end his problems were still there, the same as they were when he came. But something had changed in him, something had deepened, and so he saw his situation differently and would live it differently.

There is always a mutuality of grace in spiritual direction. I, too, had been changed by this man's struggle, and found myself thinking more and more about surrender. The word began to appear with greater frequency in my conversations, both social and ministerial. I became more focused on the fundamental importance of this stance in the spiritual life, and explored the different ways that surrender was expressed by both the classical Christian writers and by the saints. I tried to become more aware of the power and feel of surrender, and began to recognize the tight, closed-up feeling of those unyielded moments when I had in some way said "no" to God.

Yet it means little to simply think about surrender, or read a book about it, or even write one. In the final analysis, it is actively *living out* surrender that matters, *choosing* to surrender to God not in some abstract, ethereal way, but in the concrete circumstances of any given moment. That's when surrender becomes real, or not; that's when we step forward in love, or not.

Presumably, you are reading these words because something about the concept of spiritual surrender attracts you.

Perhaps you scanned the table of contents and connected with the theme of one of the chapters. Maybe you've been experiencing an inner tug that calls you to give yourself more completely to the Divine Lover.

Maybe you are going through a difficult time in your life, struggling with illness or addiction in yourself or in someone you care about. Perhaps you hope to deepen your prayer life. However it is that you have come to hold this book, let us both agree on this: it is to be judged of worth only to the degree that it furthers your actual practice of surrender to God. That is my reason for writing it; may it be your reason for reading.

At the end of each chapter you will find a section called "For Your Prayer," intended to help you connect what has been discussed in the chapter to your own life experience in Christ. These prayer exercises use different approaches—biblical reflection, guided imagery, and prayer with memories— to best reflect the content of the material in the chapter. They are presented here for individual use, but can also be used well with a group of people (particularly the prayers that use guided imagery).

Some of these prayer exercises may appeal to you more than others, and in this I know of no better advice than that cardinal rule of prayer: if it works for you, use it, and if it doesn't, don't. But you will find it of value to bring the theme of each chapter in this book to prayer in some way before reading on, for nothing can move an insight from page to practice better than prayer. And after all, we have no greater teacher in learning surrender than the One whom we meet in prayer.

CHAPTER 1

THE MEANING OF SURRENDER

What comes to mind when you hear the word "surrender"? Many people associate the word with military battles, or struggles of other kinds. In this regard surrender means to quit, to stop the effort and give up trying. It implies being a loser. It's no surprise, then, that the word can evoke a negative response. We live in a madly competitive society, and are raised to strive for dominance and victory in every arena—sports, business, academics, war. When winning is everything, surrender can be a dirty word.

Others think of surrender as a kind of passive resignation that simply accepts everything as it is: "que sera, sera/whatever will be, will be." Such a fatalistic approach can be a convenient way of absolving oneself from any responsibility: "That's just the way life is." "Don't let yourself be bothered by it." "You can't fight city hall." "Take what comes and don't make waves." Sometimes this attitude is presented as being very spiritual. But in fact, this philosophy of life can be an easy cover for laziness and cowardice.

For some, the word surrender implies servility, submissiveness, and obedience to established authorities. Unfortunately, within both Church and society, the language of surrender has at times been used in this way to stifle opposition and the winds of change. What great avenues of abuse are opened then! Women and minorities rightly reject admonitions to surrender when it is thus distorted to maintain an oppressive condition.

If these are the understandings we bring to the notion of surrender, most of us would not find it very appealing. But these understandings are inadequate and misleading when speaking of spiritual surrender: we are not called to be wimps and doormats.

In fact, for the Christian, living the surrendered life often means *not* quitting, but actively persisting in worldly struggles even when we may want to stop. Living the surrendered life often means *not* accepting things as they are, but working with God to change them. Indeed, there is much that is not as it should be, both in our own lives and in the world at large. War and crime and poverty and materialism may be seen as unchangeable realities by those of no faith; but the believer has been called to proclaim God's reign among us and to act against the powers of sin and death.

Surrender sometimes calls for obedience to established authorities—but not always. We don't have to look far to find examples of men and women who, precisely because they were living surrendered lives, refused to submit to those in power. Martin Luther King, Jr., for instance, promoted nonviolent civil disobedience, led marches of protest, and openly criticized President Johnson on the war in Vietnam. Dorothy Day was also involved in nonviolent protest. She was quite willing to put herself on the front lines, and willingly accepted arrest and imprisonment. In Germany, Lutheran pastor Dietrich Bonhoeffer actively sought to overthrow the Nazi regime during World War II.

Similarly, because she was living surrender, the fourteenth-century holy woman Catherine of Siena could write bold criticism such as this to Pope Gregory XI: "I hope by the goodness of God, venerable father mine, that you will quench this perverse and perilous self-love in yourself." Gregory's successor, Urban VI, also knew the outspoken censure of this saint, even as she supported his authority as pope.

Far from always being docile and quiet, a surrendered soul can make others downright uncomfortable.

So what, then, is surrender? In the dictionary we find a number of definitions for the word, but this one comes closest to its spiritual meaning: "the yielding of one's person, forces, or possessions to another." Spiritual surrender is not passive resignation, but an active choice to place our person, forces, and possessions into the hands of God. It is a choice that undergirds all that we do, and is to be actualized in all the daily decisions we make. Surrender is yielding to God's dream for us, as this dream is made known within our lives. It is a giving over of oneself to the triune God.

Thus spiritual surrender is not like the crushing experience of surrender to an enemy which leaves us broken and shame-filled. Our God is not a general who uses brute force to coerce our submission and who delights in breaking our will. No, spiritual surrender is a deliberate act of the will, not a breaking of the will.

Our God entices, our God attracts. Certainly it can seem at times that God is irresistible, as the prophet Jeremiah testifies:

"O Lord, you have enticed me, and I was enticed; you have overpowered me, and you have prevailed" (Jer 20:7). But as Jeremiah and so many other prophets and mystics have affirmed, it is not by irresistible might that God wins our surrender but by irresistible beauty and love.

Our God pursues us in a fire of divine passion, yet "with unhurrying chase, and unperturbed pace, deliberate speed, majestic instancy," as Francis Thompson writes in his poem "The Hound of Heaven." Surrender to this God is abundantly life-giving, like surrender to a lover, with all the joy of mutual possession. In fact, spiritual surrender *is* surrender to a Lover, One who woos us with words and with gifts and will not relent until we yield to the divine seduction.

If this surrender means quitting anything, it means that we stop obstructing God's grace in our lives. If it means stopping effort, it means stopping our effort to keep the Divine Lover at arm's length. If it means losing a struggle, we lose it to One who will make this loss our greatest victory.

Surrender, then, is the fundamental act of the Christian life. Our conscious awareness of spiritual life must begin with an act of surrender, and only through our continued yielding to God, day in and day out, are we able to grow in that life.

Lives Compelled by Grace

The life of surrender may commence in circumstances as unique as each believer. St. Paul, for example, surrendered on the Damascus road after he was knocked to the ground by a blinding light and a thunderous voice. "It hurts you to kick against the goads," Jesus said to him (Acts 26:14), words that could be said to any who struggle against God's advances.

Thus, a radically new life began for Paul; from that moment on, he belonged to Christ and strove to become evermore yielded to Christ. "For his sake I have suffered the loss of all things, and I regard them as rubbish, in order that I may gain Christ and be found in him....I want to know Christ and the power of his resurrection and the sharing of his sufferings by becoming like him in his death....Not that I have already obtained this or have already reached the goal; but I press on to make it my own, because Christ Jesus has made me his own" (Phil 3:8–12).

St. Margaret of Cortona was a thirteenth-century Christian who lived in Tuscany. As a young woman Margaret fled her father's house to live as the pampered mistress of a wealthy nobleman. She scandalized the townspeople by taking up residence in his castle and bearing him a son. She lived in luxury with the nobleman for nine years, until he was murdered one day on a ride through the woods. Margaret's moment of surrender happened when she viewed the corpse of her dead lover: she made a decision to belong henceforth to Christ. Her subsequent life of charity, prayer, and selflessness astonished all who had previously known her.

Ignatius of Loyola (1492-1556) surrendered in a hospital bed. Like many of the saints, he was anything but a saint in his youth, which was filled with violence, gambling, and licentiousness. But while serving in the ranks of King Charles of Spain, he had his legs literally shot out from under him. With plenty of time in recuperation to read, think, and look at his life more clearly, Ignatius experienced the invitation of God and made a choice to belong to Christ.

Sometimes, it takes a drastic turn of events to move a soul to surrender. Others learn surrender at an early age, or have a subtle moment of conversion. Saints like Teresa of Avila, John of the Cross, and Thérèse of Lisieux started their spiritual journeys at an early age, growing steadily and surely in holiness.

Similarly, our own experience of surrender may follow any number of patterns. Some of us may give ourselves to God with a breathtaking suddenness. For others, it may happen slowly, as when a man and a woman are acquaintances for years and pass almost imperceptibly into the fire of romance. Still again, some of us may fiercely resist God's allurements for nearly a lifetime, even manifesting an outward antipathy toward religious faith, until one day our longing breaks through and grace wins our hearts. (Thankfully, the patience and persistence of the Divine Lover knows no bounds.)

But whoever we are and however it happens, if we have truly yielded to God, we will be who God calls us to be and live as God calls us to live. We will approach all our decisions without presuming what the better path would be, without eliminating certain paths beforehand. Statements such as "I want to belong totally to you, my God, as long as I can still earn enough money to maintain this life-style," or "I will do whatever you ask of me Lord, but don't ask me to stop drinking," have no place in an attitude of surrender.

Surrender means embracing the conviction that the better path is always that one to which God leads us. If we have been made to be a husband or wife, it would be infidelity to live as a celibate. If we know in our heart of hearts that God calls us to church ministry, we would be unfaithful if we decided instead to go into business—and vice versa. Surrender is the inner stance from which discernment flows.

Therefore, it is not the trappings of religion that mark the depth of a surrendered life. Just as an accountant may embody profound holiness, so a bishop may have yielded little to divine love. We cannot know if a particular woman's choice for the convent is a response to God's call or an avoidance of it. We cannot know if a man has chosen to work the family farm as a way of living surrender or as a way of eluding it. Who can evaluate the intention of surrender in another's life? It is hard enough to know what is going on in our own hearts!

Sometimes, remembering an experience of grace renews its effect in us; telling it to another can spread the grace around. How good it is to "boast in the Lord" as St. Paul advises us (1 Cor 1:31). It is both good for our own spirit and for those who hear it; they can then taste through us yet another flavor of divine goodness, and fall more deeply in love with God. "I will thank you forever, because of what you have done. In the presence of the faithful I will proclaim your name, for it is good" (Ps 52:9).

Yet while we celebrate the variety of our stories, what matters most is not how we first came to spiritual surrender, but that we did come to it. All of us on the Christian journey have, in varying degrees, already surrendered to God; all of us, having tasted this surrender, will want to do so more completely.

But all of us, too, are good at holding back. All of us have whole reserves of self that remain unyielded, firmly clutched in our own hands; it's part of the human condition that no one can force a complete surrender. Only Jesus, the sinless one, lived totally surrendered to God.

For the rest of us, surrender usually deepens gradually, in dribs and drabs. It is furthered in little choices that perhaps no one even sees, in little inward acts of self-abandonment. Though we may, on occasion, engage in struggles with God that leave us gasping on the floor, these generally are few and far between. It's in the nitty-gritty of day-to-day existence that our surrender becomes real; it's here that we keep making the choice to belong to God, or not.

FOR YOUR PRAYER

Use this reflection to help you focus on a time of saying "yes," then of saying "no" to God, and on the consequences of each of these actions. First, take a few moments to become silent and aware of God's presence.

Turn back very gently in memory to a time and circumstance in your life when you said "yes" to God. This may be a major turning point in your life, or it may have been a small occurrence, seemingly insignificant.

Seek to reenter that moment. Remember what was going on in your life at the time. What led up to that moment? What were the results of that "yes" to God?

Now turn back to a time and circumstance in which you said "no" to God. Once again, seek to reenter that moment in your life, and remember what was going on at the time. What led up to that moment? What were the results of that "no" to God?

What is God's invitation to you right now, at this point in your life? Ask for the grace to say "yes."

CHAPTER 2

ACCEPTING OUR CREATUREHOOD

From the beginning, we human beings have had a hard time accepting the fact that we are creatures. Although we have the exalted privilege of being made in the image and likeness of God, we are still *made*—that is, we have come into existence at the wish of Another—and we continue in existence only because God makes it so. This state of dependency and limitation continually arouses our fierce resistance. Yet accepting our creaturehood is fundamental to spiritual surrender.

The Book of Genesis tells how, in their paradisal state, Adam and Eve lived at peace with the Creator, nature, and themselves. The earliest scenes from the Bible are a picture of bliss: the animals, the lush plant life, the joy of the man and woman in having each other, and the playfulness of God in bringing good things to them. But this idyllic picture disappears when our first parents listen to the serpent's voice:

Now the serpent was more crafty than any other wild animal that the Lord God had made. He said to the woman, "Did God say, 'You shall not eat from any tree in the garden'?" The woman said to the serpent, "We may eat of the fruit of the trees in the garden; but God said, 'You shall not eat of the fruit of the tree that is in the middle of the garden, nor shall you touch it, or you shall die.'" But the serpent said to the woman, "You will not die; for God knows that when you eat of it your eyes will be opened, and you will be like God, knowing good and evil." So when the woman saw that the tree was good for food, and that it was a delight to the eyes, and that the tree was to be desired to make one wise, she took of its fruit and ate; and she also gave some to her husband, who was with her, and he ate. Then the eyes of both were opened, and they knew that they were naked; and they sewed fig leaves together and made loincloths for themselves.

They heard the sound of the Lord God walking in the garden at the time of the evening breeze, and the man and his wife hid themselves from the presence of the Lord God among the trees of the garden. (Gen 3:1–8)

"You will be like God," the serpent said. Adam and Eve embraced that empty promise, ignored God's Word, and made a choice that threw everything out of order. The harmony they had enjoyed with their fellow creatures was ended. Even their harmony with one another was disrupted. They hasten in shame to cover their nakedness, the very organs which mark man and woman as begotten, finite, created. Then, in fear they hide from the Lord God, uncomfortable now with who they are, alienated from themselves and thus from the One who made them.

"You will be like God," the serpent had promised them, like

God, and not creatures subject to Another. "You will be like God," the serpent said, in control and totally independent. Yes, it was an attractive offer, and it resounds as a strong and constant voice of temptation from that primeval garden to our own day.

Throughout history, countless souls and even whole societies have been led into misery by the temptation to be "like God." Yet the goal of this quest—to be like God—is an illusion, for although God has made "humankind in our image, according to our likeness" (Gen 1:26), we are not God—nor can we ever be. We are utterly dependent on Another, and on one another. We are creatures, not Creator, formed from the dust of the earth. (Our "earthy" origin is emphasized three times in Scripture, Gen 2:7, 3:19, and 3:23.) That we are not God is basic to our human identity.

Likewise, in the various mythic accounts of the fall of the angels, we see heavenly beings who reject their created nature to grasp at the throne of God. Milton's *Paradise Lost* depicts Satan as rejecting the idea that angels were made by God; Satan claims that angels are "self-begot," and thus divine in their own right.

According to Christian tradition, prior to the fall of the angels Satan utters the defiance that echoes through every act of sin: I will not serve. I will not name you my God. I will not submit to you. I will not surrender. We enact that same defiance when we say "I will not serve,"and turn our face from the poor we might have helped. "I will not name you my God," we say, when we toss aside the gospel message in the name of practicality. "I will not submit to you. I will not surrender," we say, when we close out grace and seek to singlehandedly manage our own destiny.

Like the story of Adam and Eve, the story of the angels' fall from heaven illustrates the fall from joy that happens whenever creatures refuse to accept creaturehood. Now, we may think it absurd that any of us would actually deny creaturehood: it is so obviously the truth of our being. This denial, however, does not usually happen on an intellectual or philosophical level, but in the specificity of our individual lives. It is not creaturehood in the abstract that we reject, but the creaturehood found in our limitations, our inability to be someone—or something—other than who we are.

For example, when we nurture anger and resentment in ourselves because we may not have the talents or the intellect of another, we reject our creaturehood. When we hear a gifted friend play the piano, and become despondent because we cannot do the same rather than enjoying his or her virtuosity, we deny the value of our own charisms. Listening to a brilliant lecture might activate an inner accuser: "What's wrong with you? Why can't you do that?" Envy is fueled when we are unable to accept the particular creaturely limitations that are ours.

Similarly, when we will not embrace the body type and appearance we have been given, we reject our creaturehood. One woman told me how she was plagued from her youth with self-hatred, because in her view she "didn't have a pretty face" and was always battling obesity. For years she was openly negative about God and religion, even mocking people who talked seriously about it. "I didn't know it then, but I was blaming God for making me like this," she said. "Now I've stopped measuring myself against Madison Avenue images of womanhood. I can see the real beauty I have, and I can accept that it may not be the same beauty others have. God and I are good friends now."

As this woman's story illustrates, the rejection of creaturehood, however it might be manifested, inevitably turns us against the One who made us the way we are. When we despise our particular limitations and contingency, we easily become hostile to the One deemed responsible. Much anger toward God grows from this nonacceptance of ourselves. Like the angelic rebels, out of spite we may even turn away from our Creator completely.

Finite creatures that we are, we cannot have and be all things. Our genetic makeup, the concrete historical circumstances of our family and upbringing, the specifics of the geographical and cultural environment we are born into—all these create for us certain opportunities as well as certain limitations that are inherent to our creaturehood. The events and the people that make up our personal history are irrevocably part of who we are, as are any innate disabilities or gifts.

Accepting our creaturehood means putting our energies into living happily and fruitfully within our limitations, not into fighting against them. To be sure, there are difficulties and obstacles in any life that can and should be overcome. But even so, we will still face conditions and situations within our lives that are unalterable.

Surrender means accepting the fact that we are creatures, not God—what relief and peace such surrender brings! It means that we don't have to always be "in charge." We don't have to be responsible for every detail of life around us, for every outcome of every situation. God will let us know what is ours to attend to.

Addiction

The twelve-step program of Alcoholics Anonymous and related groups has been extremely successful in turning people's lives around. Step one on the journey to healing and wholeness is to admit powerlessness and give up the illusion of being in control.

The person seeking freedom is then invited to look to Higher Power, understood by most people as God, and to

make a decision to turn his or her life over to the care of this
Higher Power. Though for anyone, of course, this admission
and decision must be repeated on a daily basis, the process of
breaking the bonds of addiction can only go forward when
these first steps are taken. "First things first," the program
teaches. "Let go and let God."

This first step in the program recognizes that many people
initially come to be addicted through the quest for something
to take them beyond their limitations, something that will
make them more godlike. If Joe is living with a painful sense
of personal inadequacy, alcohol may create for him the illusion
that he is more clever, more witty, and more sexually appealing. For Marsha, drinking may provide a way to simply with-
draw to a numbed state where no one and nothing can hurt
her.

Ned's cocaine use frees him from having to face problems
in the family and on the job, while Sandra's compulsive gambling is fed by the excitement of risk that lifts her above the
routine of day-to-day existence. Elaine's sex addiction makes
her feel powerful and desirable; Tom's addiction to sex is a
way of feeling lovable when deep down he can't believe he
really is.

Those who care about the addict can get caught up in the
disease in their own way. Codependent family members and
friends may try to control the behavior of the addicted person,
acting out of the fantasy that they can make the addict stop.
One woman tells of how she scrubbed her house daily for
years, compulsively and meticulously cleaning every nook
and cranny in the belief that if the house were "really nice" her
husband wouldn't go out drinking at night. A man tells of the
fortune he spent on jewelry, vacations, and expensive clothes,
all purchased for his wife in the naive hope that if she had
"lots of pretty things" she wouldn't need alcohol.

When one strategy of control doesn't work, the codependent may adopt another, and still another. But the inner assumption remains the same: "I can manage this other person's behavior. I have the power. In this I can be like God." If the alcoholic must often "hit bottom" before facing the truth, sometimes it takes hitting bottom for the codependent, too. Both must accept that they are limited creatures, and be able to say to themselves, "There is a God, and it's not me."

For addicted and codependent persons alike, then, recovery begins with a recognition of powerlessness and the choice to surrender to a Higher Power. It begins with an acknowledgment that the only source of true self-worth is right relationship with God, not something "out there" whether that be chemicals, food, gambling, or sex.

Yet here, too, surrender does not mean passivity. Having yielded initially to a Higher Power, the person in recovery does not sit back and wait for God to miraculously fix everything. A great deal of work lies ahead on the difficult road to renewal, and anyone not willing to do it has not really surrendered. But paradoxically, admitting creaturely powerlessness actually empowers the soul to follow through: "So, I will boast all the more gladly of my weaknesses, so that the power of Christ may dwell in me....for whenever I am weak, then I am strong" (2 Cor. 12:9–10).

I have seen the transforming effect of this many times in the lives of men and women I've served in spiritual direction, who have found in surrender freedom from various addictions. Indeed, some of the most spiritual people I know have come to holiness by way of addiction. It's not a path anyone would choose, to be sure.

But over and over again I have heard people in recovery tell of how much better they have become by coming through such hell. One man even exclaimed "O happy fault!" that brought him, finally, to the arms of God. Perhaps people who have not experienced such darkness find it too easy to live in the illusion of having control. How fortunate are those who can choose the surrendered life without being driven into it!

Perfectionism

For all of us, accepting the fact that we are creatures will include one very important element: letting go of perfectionism. To be God is to be perfect. But to be a creature is to be imperfect, limited, and vulnerable. To be a creature is to be in process, not yet complete—at least not on this side of the grave.

Yet so many of us are harassed by a little inner voice that keeps telling us, "You must be flawless." Wherever this subconscious message originates, too often we mistake it for the voice of God. Then we knock ourselves out trying to live up to it, and feel like we are a failure and a disappointment to God because we cannot be perfect. But that harassing voice is not the voice of our Creator: it's just a replay of the age-old Genesis temptation, "you will be like God" (and we know the results of listening to that voice!).

The voice of perfectionism induces guilt in us when we fall short of unrealistic standards of what it means to be a parent or a spouse or a devoted son or daughter. It chastises us because we can't entirely control our own lives, or our children's lives, or our coworkers' lives. The voice of perfectionism holds us personally responsible when everything doesn't work out just right. It stirs us to berate ourselves because we are finite, to fight against our own limited humanity, and even to hate this human nature that God, in Jesus, chose to assume.

No, the voice of perfectionism is not the voice of God, and when we hear that voice inside us we need to talk back to it. A friend of mine tells how she spent much of her life trying to satisfy that voice, and of course, never succeeding. She shared how several years ago she finally caught on to what was happening, and made a New Year's resolution not to be superwoman anymore. From then on, whenever the drive to perfectionism flared up, she simply stopped and reminded herself "I don't have to be superwoman." That simple practice brought about a revolutionary change in her life. She was able to accept her limitations and imperfection, and let God be God in her world.

I wrestle with perfectionism, too, and consciously talk back to that critical inner voice. Sometimes, humor is the best antidote to perfectionism. When I begin to get uptight about my failures and foibles, I try to laugh rather than scold myself. "Here I go again, Lord," I pray. "Isn't it funny the way I take myself and my work so seriously? Help me to love and accept myself, broken as I am, the way you love and accept me."

Like a rampant virus, perfectionism can spread through contact with people infected with it. Many of us begin along this path by internalizing the real or imagined expectations of others who are important to us: mother, father, siblings, spouse, teachers, mentors, ministers, or friends. Eager not to disappoint this person we care about, we struggle to be who she wants us to be, or do it the way he wants us to do it. We may never even consider whether or not this person's expectations are reasonable or doable. In the end, when our efforts win criticism or scant praise, we become more determined to get it right the next time, and thus continue the cycle of perfectionism.

If we can "catch" and internalize another's perfectionism, so, too, can we become freer through contact with a surrendered soul. How liberating it is when we encounter someone who gives us permission to be the imperfect creatures we are! No doubt there are many such people in each of our lives.

I'll never forget how one day, in the early weeks of my marriage, I was in a particularly bad mood. I didn't want to talk to anyone, and was sullen and irritated for no apparent reason. After snapping at my wife, I immediately realized my insensitivity, and apologized profusely. My wife simply smiled. "It's okay to have a crabby day," she said. "Don't worry about it; I'll stay out of your way, and you do what you need to do to feel better." I was astonished: Okay to have a crabby day? Okay to be not always smiling and cheerful? Her response was an experience of unconditional acceptance that enabled me to better accept myself.

When we experience such acceptance through another, or offer it to another, it is a revelation of the tender love of God, who "knows how we are made; [and] remembers that we are dust" (Ps 103:13–14).

Yet almost daily I hear good Christian men and women berate themselves for not being perfect. Maybe they forgot a loved one's birthday, or fell again into a habitual sin: "I can't believe what a jerk I am." "I'm such a stupid idiot for missing that." They speak words to themselves that they would never speak to another in the same circumstances. Addressed to themselves, they may assume that these words are a sign of humility.

But let us not deceive ourselves: true humility is characterized both by honest self-appraisal and graced self-acceptance. We may very well have a keen insight into our brokenness, but if our insight causes us to despise ourselves we are not being humble. Or, we may accept ourselves, but only because we refuse to look at our sins. Neither stance is spiritually healthy. In humility we both see and embrace who we are. Does not the perfect God love us in our imperfection?

Of course, letting go of perfectionism doesn't mean that we stop trying to improve. As Christians, we always seek to "grow up in every way into him who is the head, into Christ" (Eph 4:15). Letting go of perfectionism means accepting that often our very best still leaves room for improvement, and probably always will. That's what creaturehood is all about.

So give up the drive to be limitless! Stop viewing your creaturely limitations as obstacles to holiness when they are, indeed, the *means* to holiness. Don't compete with God for omnipotence: let go of perfectionism, and surrender.

FOR YOUR PRAYER

God loves us in our imperfections, even when we ourselves are loathe to acknowledge them. To begin this reflection, read 2 Cor 12:7–10. Then quiet yourself and become aware of the presence of God.

All of us, no doubt, have "thorns" that we feel are obstacles to our spiritual growth. Take a few moments to identify and think about one such problem in your life that you have been able to overcome and grow through. It may be an illness or personality trait, a family situation or circumstance of birth. It may be anything that you saw as a limitation to be overcome and conquered.

Reflect on how your life has changed now that you are free (or freer) of this thorn.

We also have thorns that remain as limitations in our lives despite our prayer and best efforts. Take a few moments to identify and think about one such persistent "problem" in your life.

Consider before God whether this might be, not an obstacle to growth, but an occasion for grace. Reflect on the possibility that in the providence of God, this thorn may serve some important, salvific purpose for yourself or others.

In closing, ask for the grace to see all your thorns as God sees them.

CHAPTER 3

SURRENDER IN SUFFERING

Suffering inevitably comes to all of us. We may be moving happily through our days, and then a loved one is torn from us, or a spot on an X-ray destroys our sense of security. An ache, once easy to ignore, becomes intolerably intense and chronic. A cherished relationship breaks down, and now the presence of one who once brought joy produces tension and mistrust. We suffer through major surgery and the pain of convalescence, or sit by the sickbed of a spouse or child or friend, one with them in their agony.

Suffering is like an uninvited and unwelcome visitor at our door. We feel unprepared for this invading presence, which disrupts our plans, interferes with our rest, and demands our attention. Its coming and going is unpredictable. It may leave us, only to return at the most inconvenient times, or it may just stay on to become a permanent, bothersome companion.

Whatever form it takes—physical, mental, emotional, or spiritual—suffering presents a challenge to faith, and often strains our relationship with God. Yet at the same time it provides us with an opportunity to move into ever deeper levels of surrender.

The reality of suffering stirs up persistent, yet often unanswerable questions within us. Even if we have never been prone to doubts before, when we suffer, we question—and it seems that the greater the suffering, the greater the questioning. What does divine Providence mean, when I am allowed such pain? Is God's love real? What good is an Almighty whose might will not ease my suffering?

We read in Scripture of God's protection: "You will not fear the terror of the night, or the arrow that flies by day, or the pestilence that stalks in darkness, or the destruction that wastes at noonday. A thousand may fall at your side, ten thousand at your right hand, but it will not come near you" (Ps 91:5–7). How can I believe in One who promises this, yet does not seem to deliver?

But above all, we question, why? Why did God take my husband? Why do I have to live with this disease? Why did God let my boss humiliate me before my peers and then fire me? "Why do you forget our affliction and oppression?" "Why have you forsaken me?" "Why must I walk mournfully because of the oppression of the enemy?" (Ps 44:24, 22:1, 43:2)

Theologians and philosophers have wrestled with this question forever; their books and treatises fill libraries as testimony to their efforts to make sense of suffering. Yet the human mind is ultimately humbled in the attempt. Suffering remains a mystery. It is, as a monk once phrased it to me, "the atheist's only valid argument." For although explanations abound, there is none that is totally adequate.

One common approach views suffering as a punishment for something we have done. "I lost my baby because I had an affair." "My father was taken from me because I never appreciated him." "I have this cancer because I've been such a selfish person." The assumption that suffering is a punishment also underlies statements like, "What have I done to deserve this?" or "It's not fair—I've always tried to live a good life!" But from a Christian perspective, suffering is not a punishment for personal sin. Jesus specifically rejects this belief, and we should too (see Lk 13:1–5 or Jn 9:1–3).

Another prevalent way people attempt to explain suffering is to say that God sends it to teach us something. "I keep telling God 'I know now what you wanted me to learn. Bring this to an end.'" "I must not have learned yet what I'm supposed to learn." A third way simply ascribes a specific reason for it. "God must have taken my husband so I'd be free for my ministry." "Perhaps I fell and broke my back because God wanted me to have more time for prayer."

Each of these explanations presumes that suffering is God's doing, and so we have to find a way to justify God for doing it. But what if suffering isn't God's doing at all? What if God didn't "take" my husband or baby, didn't "send" my cancer, or accident, or chronic pain? What if God never actively wills our suffering? What if God is as averse to human suffering as we are ourselves?

This more positive image of God is, in fact, closer to revealed truth, and so discounts the above explanations for suffering. Yet even so, the questions remain. Why does God allow my pain if God does not really want human suffering?

Perhaps the search for explanations, while natural for our questing minds, is destined to frustration. What explanation can ease human suffering anyway? What theory will transform our experience of it? While our intellects must ever search for reasons, when suffering comes it is not by understanding that we find growth. When suffering comes, it is surrender that makes all the difference.

A Transformative Act

Jesus is our model of surrender in suffering. We see him in Gethsemane, betrayed by a friend and sweating blood at the thought of what awaited him. Yet his prayer was one of surrender: "Remove this cup from me; yet, not my will but yours be done" (Lk 22:42).

Did Jesus want to go to the cross? Not according to the gospel. Would any healthy man in the prime of life want to be tortured and killed? In a perfect example of open honesty in prayer, Jesus told his *Abba* what he wanted: he wanted the cup of suffering to be taken from him. Even so, he yielded himself to God: "not my will but yours be done." Of course he wanted to be spared, but he wanted even more to live God's call.

How hard such surrender is in the midst of suffering! It is not romantic or easy, so we need not berate ourselves when we find surrender to God hard to attain. The son of God himself did not live it peacefully and without struggle, but in agony and loneliness, and "with loud cries and tears" (Heb 5:7). We may well find ourselves lamenting with Jesus, and feeling forsaken, even as we pray with him "into your hands..."
(Mk 15:34, Lk 23:46).

I once knew a holy woman who was in the final throes of a long battle with stomach cancer. When she was first diagnosed, she had resolved to move through the stages of her illness with courage and calm, as a witness to the presence of God in her life.

Instead, as the disease progressed she found she was no different from the other patients. More often than not, she was not strong, but weak. She, too, trembled before the shadowed face of death and wept in the quiet of the night. Yet her greatest fear was that somehow her surrender to the Divine Lover was only halfhearted. Why else was she so unable to find contentment in pain?

While she thus questioned, all of us who knew her saw and tes-
tified to what was apparently hidden from her own eyes. We felt
the power and the depth of her surrender in suffering. Family and
friends and medical staff alike were moved, and at least one person was converted by her evident sanctity. She died in peace, and
I believe that in her final moments she was aware of how completely she belonged to God and God to her.

Spiritual surrender should not be viewed, then, as providing a
pious escape from the reality of suffering. It does not mean that we
will be spared what others must endure, or be able to glide
through the worst on a cloud of tranquillity. It did not mean this
for Jesus, who was utterly yielded to his Father, and it will not
mean this for us.

In the divine economy, the pain of life which is part of our creaturely existence can be used by God for our own liberation and for
the redemption of the world. Though we may never come to
understand a reason for our suffering, in surrender it can have
meaning and serve a purpose.

As we yield to God in the midst of suffering, we ourselves are
purified, sanctified, and more profoundly united with Christ.
Others will be affected by it as well. If, as Scripture says of
Jesus,"by his bruises we are healed" (1 Pt 2:24), in him our bruises, too, can take on a redemptive significance. Our surrender in
suffering radiates a healing light for the world, the healing light
who is Christ.

But only in surrender can suffering take on such salvific power.
Without it, suffering tends only to embitter us, and depress others.
We become joyless and despairing; we turn away from God.
Enclosed in our own night of pain, we brood on our crosses as if
to "suck the last drops of disappointment out of them," to borrow
a phrase of Evelyn Underhill. Friedrich von Hügel, an English
spiritual writer who was the mentor and spiritual director of
Underhill, called this pain "being cross with our crosses."

When we offer our pain for a specific person or cause, our suffering becomes transformed—and transformative—in Jesus. As a child, you may have been told, as I was, to "offer it up" when pain or difficulties came your way. While these words have become trite, almost a joke to some, they represent sound spiritual advice. To "offer it up" is an act of surrender. It is a way of turning from self-absorption to othercenteredness. It enacts a fundamental Christian insight, namely, that one's suffering can have a salutary effect on another.

This concept was beautifully expressed by an elderly woman whom I know. She is plagued with a circulatory ailment which causes her frequent bouts of excruciating leg pain. When the pain came, she would lie down on her bed, often wishing to die rather than to have such suffering.

One day, during a particularly difficult episode, she called on the name of Jesus, and pictured him on the cross. Then she made an act of surrender. As the woman herself told me, "I gave my pain to Jesus, and asked him to unite it with his own. I thought of the family I loved, and asked him to let my pain become a prayer for them—and, you know, something changed. It wasn't that the pain got any better. But something changed in me." She half-smiled as she said, "When I offered it up to him, I felt less sorry for myself, less like a victim. I began to believe that I could still do some good in this world, if only through my offered suffering."

As this woman experienced, surrender in suffering moves us from a stance of self-pitying victimhood to one of active participation in the saving work of Christ. Our self-identity and even our sense of self-worth shifts. We begin to see ourselves as someone who is doing something positive with a bad situation, turning the lead of suffering into the gold of service through the alchemy of spiritual surrender. St. Paul wrote that "in my flesh I am completing what is lacking in Christ's afflictions" (Col 1:24); likewise, our sufferings, senseless though they may seem, can become a force for good in the world through surrender.

In December of 1994, my wife Debra gave birth to James Adam, our fourth child. As the labor progressed along its normal course, the pains became more and more intense for her. Toward the end, when my wife's contractions were at their hardest and she was in the depths of her suffering, one of the nurses who assisted us began softly repeating a phrase to her, like a prayer, a mantra: "Let the pain open you up. Let the pain open you up."

These are words of profound wisdom, not only for the process of childbirth, but for all of life. In childbirth, those difficult contractions are meant to open the womb for the delivery of the baby. A woman can fight against it, but to do so is only to make it harder on herself and on the child. When she lets the pain open her, new life is born into the world.

Let the pain open you up! Whatever the nature of the suffering that we must endure, we can choose to suffer it in a way that enlarges us and is life-giving, or in a way that closes us down and makes us small. The key is to surrender, in Christ and with Christ. As Jesus prayed, "Let it be..."; as Jesus prayed, "Into your hands...."

Nonphysical Suffering

Of the many forms of suffering, physical pain is perhaps the most obvious. But emotional, mental, and spiritual suffering are just as real, and can be even more terrible. Hidden pain, like anxiety, worry, guilt, or hopelessness, is every bit as real as the gut pain of an ulcer. The shame and self-loathing that often accompany addictive behaviors can create a seemingly inescapable hell for those caught in an addiction. Some people caught in the black pit of depression have told me that they would gladly trade this condition for a broken arm or two.

Though nonphysical suffering often accompanies the physical, sometimes it appears alone, perhaps when we are in the peak of physical health.

When our suffering is not a suffering of the body it is often compounded by the aloneness we feel in carrying it. Everyone jumps to our assistance when we are bedridden with the flu, or hobbling on crutches. But since our inner pain is usually unseen, it can go unaided.

Further, if we do not speak of our inner pain to another out of embarrassment or fear, we may make the situation worse for ourselves. Telling of our suffering to at least one trusted person—family member, friend, spiritual director, counselor—is itself an important movement toward surrender. St. Ignatius of Loyola recognizes this in one of the rules for discernment from his Spiritual Exercises, when he speaks of how secrecy about inner turmoil only enables it to grip us more tightly:

> ...when the enemy of human nature [Satan] turns his wiles and persuasions upon an upright person, he intends and desires them to be received and kept in secrecy. But when the person reveals them to his or her good confessor or some other spiritual person who understands the enemy's deceits and malice, he [Satan] is grievously disappointed. For he quickly sees that he cannot succeed in the malicious project he began, because his manifest deceptions have been detected.

While Ignatius is here speaking specifically of the torment of temptation, his wisdom applies as well to all kinds of inner suffering.

To tell someone of our unseen pain is an acknowledgment of creaturely brokenness that enables grace to have greater scope in us. To tell someone of our unseen pain is an act of

— invite disciples

opening up, of yielding control. Not a few times I have sat with someone who was bringing to light something long borne in silence; not a few times I have gone through the process myself. I know it can be agonizingly difficult. But I cannot think of a single instance when the revelation of inner suffering has not brought some relief to the burdened soul.

Just to have someone with whom we can be authentic can *authentic* be a great relief. It takes a great deal of energy to always act as if nothing were wrong, when in fact we may be feeling as if there were a worm gnawing at our insides. Being able to let down and say to someone "No, everything is *not* all right" can give us a better handle on our situation.

Inner pain can distort our perspective on life and on ourselves. We can get so caught in the misery within us that we no longer see clearly. For example, our horrific sense of guilt may be way out of proportion to the offense, or anxiety over a perceived threat may blind us to the simple steps we can take to avert a problem. Similarly, we may be consumed with a self-perpetuating worry that has little or no basis in fact. When we confide such sufferings to another, we can gain an objective point of view through that person's eyes which in itself can be healing.

The redemptive power of surrender in suffering is no less when our pain is of a nonphysical kind. Jesus himself knew the whole gamut of mental, emotional, and spiritual suffering—except sin—and these sufferings, no less than the bodily pain he endured, are part of the sacrifice that we now call saving. So we need not hesitate to offer him our depression, fear, grief, or worry, or even our remorse over personal sin. Insofar as we let him, Jesus will carry these sufferings with us and render them fruitful in God.

Compassion
There is yet another kind of suffering that must be addressed.

This is the pain we feel when another is in pain. It can be the personal grief of witnessing the suffering of someone near to us, or the collective heartache of listening to the daily news with its reports of human agony from all around the earth. This kind of suffering is both a result of our surrender and an occasion for surrender.

It is a result of our surrender because in giving ourselves to God we cannot help but be sensitized to other human beings. As we are drawn by grace into the heart of God, we find inscribed there all the joys and sorrows of humanity. And although some use religion as an escape or anesthetic, those who think they can escape a pain-filled world by turning to God will be frustrated in the attempt. Our God is compassionate, and intimacy with God generates compassion in us.

The word "compassion" means "to suffer with," or "to bear with." Indeed, the depth of our surrender is reflected in the depth of our compassion—the link is unbreakable. "Those who say, 'I love God,' and hate their brothers or sisters, are liars; for those who do not love a brother or sister whom they have seen, cannot love God whom they have not seen" (1 Jn 4:20). There is no such thing as a hardhearted saint.

Yet we can still choose to close our eyes and ears, and not let ourselves be moved by the cries of another. Many make that choice each day, out of self-centeredness or for self-protection. But we must recognize this choice for what it is, one that at once closes out the suffering brother or sister, and God: "I was hungry and you gave me no food, I was thirsty and you gave me nothing to drink, I was a stranger and you did not welcome me, naked and you did not give me clothing, sick and in prison and you did not visit me" (Mt 25:42–43).

This well-known list could be expanded endlessly to encompass all the afflictions of the human family: "I was raped...I was an abused child...I was the aborted baby...I was the damaged mother...I was your friend with cancer...I was the alcoholic...I was the victim of discrimination..." and so on. The refrain ever remains the same: "just as you did it to one of the least of these who are members of my family, you did it to me" (Mt 25:40).

In surrender, we choose to let ourselves be affected by other people's pain, and choose to respond in mercy. It is the way of Christ, who as God could have ignored our plight, but chose instead to take it on and transform it. Of course, we are not God, and we cannot carry all the world's sufferings or touch all its wounds. Though one individual can do much to alleviate human anguish, there are personal limits which must be carefully discerned by each of us. If we take on too much we may find ourselves paralyzed by an overload of grief and despair.

Yet as we grow in Christ, our capacity for creatively suffering with another grows as well. Francis of Assisi was sickened by the sight of lepers, but he came in due time to love and serve them. Early in his spiritual journey, God had said to him, "What once you found bitter will become sweet"; this was realized in Francis's experience.

The same can happen for us as we surrender to our God. We, too, may find ourselves led to deeds of compassion that once would have been beyond our imagining. We, too, may be surprised to discover that sharing another's suffering in the Lord is a privilege which fills us with the deepest gratitude.

Though suffering is an unavoidable part of life, Scripture reminds us that it is not forever; it is not our ultimate destiny. The day is coming when "Death will be no more; mourning and crying and pain will be no more" (Rev 21:4), and the One who made us will tenderly wipe every tear from our eyes. St. Paul, as well, tells of how "the sufferings of this present time are not worth comparing with the glory about to be revealed to us" (Rom 8:18).

I suspect that when we reach this future state, our questions about the mystery of suffering will find, at last, their answers. Until then, when dark days come we would do well to keep before us the biblical promise of hope and certain joy, and live our lives in surrender.

FOR YOUR PRAYER

Here is a guided imagery meditation which you may find useful for approaching the mystery of the cross. After centering yourself in silence, read through the meditation below, using your imagination to reflect on the words and their meaning.

It is a gray and cloudy day. You have been walking a long time, and your legs are growing weary from the journey. The hillside you have been climbing is very steep, and now for a brief moment, you pause to survey the surrounding countryside.

All is wrapped in mist, a mist that obscures the distance, and gives the whole landscape a soft, dreamlike quality. It is very silent here on this hillside, very still. No sound comes to your ears, no breeze stirs the moist warm air.

You see that the surface of the ground where you stand is covered with footprints. You realize that untold numbers of people have come, like you, to climb this holy hill. You see footprints large and small, footprints on top of footprints. Centuries of pilgrims have made this same journey to this holy place.

It is a place from time, yet it belongs to all time. It is the holy hill of Calvary.

You resume your climb and very soon reach the crest of the hill. There before you, stark against the gray sky, is the cross of Jesus. There, before your eyes, is your brother, your savior, pinned to the wood of the cross. Take a few moments now to look at Jesus in his passion.

You notice that his eyes are upon you. Even before you gazed upon him his gaze was fixed upon you. He is looking at you, from his cross. Look into the eyes of Jesus.

Then Jesus' lips part. He speaks to you, and says simply "for you." What do you want to say to Jesus right now?

Yes, yours are the sufferings he bears, yours the sorrows he carries. Through his wounds you are healed. Now offer to Jesus crucified your sorrows or sufferings. Tell him of the areas of your life where you are hurting. Ask him to heal you. Be attentive to what he may say, or do, in response.

There is someone else you know who is also in need of Jesus' healing. Talk to Jesus now about that person.

It is nearly time for you to leave. Take a moment now to walk closer to the cross. Reach up your hand, and touch the feet of Jesus. Let your touch communicate to him how much you love him, how much you care.

Turn and begin your descent from the hill of Calvary, back into the world Jesus died for, the world where the crucified Jesus can be touched in the flesh of any who suffer. Down the misty hillside you walk.

Conclude your prayer by expressing your gratitude to Jesus for his unending sacrifice and love.

CHAPTER 4

SURRENDER IN PLEASURE AND JOY

"**A** glutton and a drunkard" is what some people called Jesus (Mt 11:19). That Jesus should have such a reputation during his lifetime would indicate that he was no desert ascetic like John the Baptist, who wore camel's hair and lived on locusts and wild honey.

No, Jesus was to be found among his people, and though he knew the spiritual value of fasting, he knew, too, the spiritual value of celebrating with food and drink and the company of good friends. Over and over again we find Jesus at dinner parties (see, for example, Luke 7:36–50, 11:37, and 14:1). According to John's gospel, Jesus' first miracle was the production of fine wine for a wedding gone dry. When a multitude was hungry in a deserted place, he wasted no time in providing a feast for them. When he was facing his death, Jesus made it clear that he wanted to be remembered in a community meal of bread and wine.

"A glutton and a drunkard" they called him, because he came eating and drinking, enjoying himself. Here is our God, laughing with his companions, maybe telling a good joke. Here is our God, savoring the flavor of foods, smelling the aromas, chewing and swallowing and knowing the satisfaction of a full belly.

To imagine our savior taking pleasure in such earthy things might seem offensive to the religious sensibilities of some, who picture a Jesus more aloof from experiences of this kind. Yet Christian tradition recognizes it is precisely in the humanity of this man from Nazareth that we encounter the eternal God. God is not aloof from us; God is incarnate, fully and personally immersed in the human condition. This incarnation has always been a scandal, but it is one we evade at our own spiritual peril.

Throughout the centuries, innumerable devotional books and prayers have focused attention on the sufferings of Jesus, often describing his torment in all its gory detail. But if we are wont to reflect on the suffering aspect of Jesus' life, should we not also reflect on the pleasure and joy which he embraced and experienced in his holy humanity?

Jesus was alive to all kinds sensory experience. As a child, he surely knew the sheer bliss of being suckled at his mother's breast, the exhilarating embrace of his father's strong arms, the comfort of falling asleep to a lullaby, warm beneath a blanket of wool.

Would he not, as well, have run with his playmates, thrilled at the speed his young body could attain? Would he not have climbed trees and wandered after an intriguing butterfly, stuck his hands in cool mud, and felt the total refreshment of swimming on a hot day? Would he not have been energized by his physical passage to manhood, and his religious and social acceptance into the community of adults?

So many of the gospel texts are suggestive of the pleasure Jesus found in being alive and being human. Who can hear Jesus speak of the lilies of the field and the birds of the air without hearing his delight in beholding them? He knows, too, the homey smell of yeasty bread, rising so mysteriously. He understands the wonder of seeing tiny seeds buried in the ground, then growing into wheat. He has felt the exuberance of finding something precious, of recovering something lost, of being filled with the Holy Spirit.

When we experience pleasure or joy, our spirit testifies that we are in touch with what life was meant to be. We sit contentedly at the ocean shore with a friend or our family on a sunny day and find ourselves saying, "This is what life is all about." We are filled with awe at the birth of a child, or burst with pride at a wedding or graduation, and know that the moment has an eternal quality about it. So, too, when we fall in love or achieve a long-sought goal.

Pleasure and joy are instinctively recognized as normal and good. When suffering comes, we ask God "Why?" We do not ask this about pleasure and joy, for they need no explanation.

Suffering is inherently transitory. Though we cannot avoid suffering in this present life, it is not part of our final future. This is not the case with pleasure and joy. These experiences in our lives are a foretaste of the life to come, a foretaste of heaven where we will know "pleasures forevermore" (Ps 16:11) and joy beyond all telling. While God does not actively will our suffering, pleasure and joy are willed, indeed.

Yet many Christian people harbor an unconscious fear that this is not so. Somewhere in our psyches lurks a suspicion that God is not pleased when we enjoy pleasures of the senses, not pleased when we are happy and know joy. Wherever it may come from—poor religious training, or something more primitive in our collective makeup—most of us would quickly repudiate such a false understanding of God. Yet it lingers still, and comes out in what people say: "Things are going so well, I'm almost afraid of what's coming." "I've been enjoying my life so much, I feel guilty."

These kinds of statements reflect belief in a God other than the One Jesus revealed. For the God of Jesus Christ does not make us pay for good things, but gives them freely and means for them to be enjoyed. There is no divine balance of blessings with disasters, no holy invoice demanding suffering for each pleasure enjoyed. We are not begrudgingly allowed our earthly pleasures by a God who turns away in distaste.

God chose to create this earth and its pleasures and the senses by which we enjoy them. More than that, our God became human, and experienced these pleasures in his own flesh, in his own human soul and spirit. Our God knows how good this life can be, and wants us to know it too.

Who would not accept and appreciate a gift from a friend, recognizing it as a sign of friendship? When we receive and cherish a gift, we receive the giver and affirm our friendship; to refuse a gift is to spurn the giver and reject the relationship. Further, it would be rude to question the motives of a friend in giving a gift, and insulting if we suspected him or her of being generous for some ulterior motive. Ideally, we accept a friend's gift in gratitude, and our happiness in receiving it makes the giver happy.

Pleasure and joy are gifts of God. To take in these gifts and savor their goodness is an act of surrender to the Divine Lover who offers them, an affirmation of the relationship between God and ourselves. We do not suspect that God has hidden motives, or shut out what God offers as if it were some kind of trick or test. We accept what is given in gratitude, knowing that God delights in our delight.

To take pleasure in the gifts of God is a mark of a saintly soul. A wonderful story told about St. Teresa of Avila illustrates this point: One day, there was a special meal being held at her convent in honor of a liturgical feast, and the main course was partridge. Teresa evidently loved partridge, for she ate her meal with such visible relish that some of her sisters were scandalized. Here was the holy Teresa taking carnal pleasure in food! To their narrow minds, it seemed so unspiritual.

As they muttered their complaints to one another, St. Teresa overheard them and responded, "Sisters, when you pray, pray. When you partridge, *partridge*!" Teresa knew that God can be honored in both fasting and feasting.

Learning to Receive God's Pleasure
In surrender, then, we become pleasure-receivers. We rejoice in our experiences of life's goodness, and let them move us toward God. They do not get in the way of our relationship with our Creator, for we recognize the giver in the gifts, and come to know and love God more through them. "For you, O Lord, have made me glad by your work; at the works of your hands I sing for joy" (Ps 92:4).

To truly be pleasure-receivers, we must give up pleasure-seeking, the hedonistic philosophy by which many people live. Pleasure-seeking is focused on self, not on relationship with God. It is motivated by the illusion that we can make ourselves happy by satisfying every appetite when it beckons. Pleasure-seeking separates the gift from the Giver, and makes it an end in itself, possessively grasping at experience for its own sake, never noticing the loving eyes of the One from whose hand it has been snatched.

While the gratification of the pleasure-seeker happens in

the isolation of his or her own ego, the surrendered soul enjoys good things in union with the God who made them. This union with God is the foundation and goal of our lives as Christians, and the reality which profoundly affects how we approach and experience suffering and sorrow, pleasure and joy. For just as any lover desires deepening union with the beloved, so too does God desire deepening union with us.

As we yield to God's desire, we belong more and more to God, in both body and spirit. "Or do you not know that your body is a temple of the Holy Spirit within you, which you have from God, and that you are not your own?" (1 Cor 6:19). The Holy Spirit—indeed, the Trinity of Divine Persons (Jn 14:15–23)—dwells within us, as a presence which permeates our entire being. St. Paul knew this oneness to such a degree that he could write "it is no longer I who live, but it is Christ who lives in me" (Gal 2:20).

Within this unity of love, God actually shares our life experience, actually knows it in us. God is not in a distant heaven dispassionately watching what we do, but right here, participating in our lives. God carries with us our sufferings and celebrates with us our joy.

This incarnational understanding is profoundly Christian, but it's not found only in Christianity. The Hindu poet Rabindranath Tagore expresses the same truth in a prayer-poem, which for many years has inspired my own reflection. He writes:

What divine drink wouldst thou have, my God, from this overflowing cup of my life?

My poet, is it thy delight to see thy creation through my eyes and to stand at the portals of my ears silently to listen to thine own eternal harmony?

Thy world is weaving words in my mind and thy joy

is adding music to them. Thou givest thyself to me in love and then feelest thine own entire sweetness in me.

What an incredible intimacy—that God should see with us through our eyes and hear with our ears! God enjoys the sweetness of the rose with us as we smell it. God relishes with us the colorful vista of a sunset as we watch it. God knows with us the sensation of rain streaming down our faces on a summer's afternoon. If surrender means receiving life's pleasures as gifts from God, it also means recognizing how deeply and truly God enjoys these gifts in us.

Sometimes, people imagine that the more spiritual we become the less attuned to this world we will be. They think that as we become more and more focused on God we will be less and less aware of what's going on around us. Eventually, they suppose, we grow beyond the pleasures of the senses and the joys of this life. We become almost otherworldy beings, who, while still here in the flesh, have already passed in spirit to the beyond.

This reflects a kind of dualism which has little place in the Christian vision. It implies that our material world is a place where God cannot be found, and ignores the truth that all things exist in God and that we ourselves "live and move and have our being" in God (Acts 17:28).

Further, the witness of the holy men and women in our tradition indicates that growth in sanctity actually heightens, not diminishes, our sensory presence to this world and our capacity to be delighted by it. (Remember St. Teresa and her partridge!) One often-noted characteristic of the great saints is that they brought a focused awareness to the people and circumstances around them. They could readily sense the needs and moods of those they lived with or served, and profoundly responded to both the sufferings and joys of the world.

In fact, the intensification of sensory awareness is a frequently reported effect of divine grace, and I have heard story after story from ordinary men and women who testify to this.

One man spoke of how, during a particularly powerful retreat week, he had sat for a while at the pond behind the retreat house: "The afternoon was perfect, and I felt like I was taking in the sunshine through every pore on my body. Then I noticed a family of ducks. It was as if I had never seen ducks before! I marveled at them, thinking what astounding creatures these birds are. I sat transfixed by the way they moved, and the sounds they made. At one point, I think I laughed right out loud, and said, 'O Lord, I love your ducks! How beautiful is your handiwork!' I'll never forget how alive I felt at that moment!"

A woman related to me how one day, as she stood grieving and praying at her son's graveside, she suddenly knew the embracing presence of God. "When I looked up, everything seemed changed, or maybe I was changed. I didn't just see the lawn that covered the hillside—I saw thousands and thousands of individual blades of grass, each one unique and distinct. I felt God in the air moving across my face. I looked up into a sky that was bluer than I could ever describe. The experience only lasted a short time, but it was very pleasurable and gave me great joy and peace."

In John's Gospel, Jesus tells of how he came so that we might have life, and have it abundantly (10:10). Are not moments like those cited above evidence of what that abundant life can mean? Do they not contain within them a promise of the pleasure and joy which will one day be ours as the ultimate fruits of surrender?

Sex and Sexuality

Sexual love is one of the most pleasurable and exhilarating of human experiences. While very much a physical act, it is almost universally recognized as a sacred moment with rich spiritual meaning and potential. The mutual self-yielding and receiving of lovemaking corresponds to the pattern of our love affair with God, and the rapturous bliss of sexual union is, according to the mystics, the nearest approximation to what total union with God is like.

Sexual surrender has, in many religious traditions, served as a metaphor for spiritual surrender. One of the most striking examples of this can be found in Hebrew Scripture, in the magnificent poem known as the Song of Songs (Song of Solomon). Though originally composed as a celebration of sexual love, Jews and Christians alike have seen in it an illustration of the relationship between the human and the divine.

From the earliest days of the Church, numerous Christian writers and saints have meditated on these lyrical and sometimes sexually explicit verses. Catherine of Siena, Teresa of Avila, and Francis de Sales found mystical meaning in the Song of Songs.

St. John of the Cross was also deeply influenced by the Song of Songs, and wrote in the same tradition, adapting popular love ballads from his time to express the realities of the spiritual life. His most famous poem, "One Dark Night," makes vivid use of sexual imagery:

> O guiding night!
> O night more lovely than the dawn!
> O night that has united
> The Lover with His beloved,
> Transforming the beloved in her Lover.
>
> Upon my flowering breast
> Which I kept wholly for him alone,
> There he lay sleeping,
> And I caressing him
> There in a breeze from the fanning cedars.

Yet very few Christians find it easy to integrate sexual expression into their spiritual lives. Sexuality seems to be an area of chronic woundedness; believers today deal with a double problem in this regard. On the one hand, we have a secular society that often seems to have lost any sense of morality about sex, trivializing it into a form of recreation. We see little in society's attitude toward sexuality that reflects the sacredness and beauty of this primary human condition.

On the other hand, the churches have inculcated in many a deep suspicion of things sexual—so much so that even married persons have told me of the guilt they feel when they engage in sexual activity with their spouses. Far from being seen as an avenue for spiritual growth, sexual love is viewed by many religious people as detrimental to union with God.

Within the Catholic tradition, we find very few examples of canonized married people for whom physical sexual expression was an integral part of their holiness. But we can rest assured that such saintly men and women did exist in abundance throughout Christian history, though their stories are not in the official church records.

It is by God's design, not by an accident of evolution, that sexual love is so wonderfully pleasurable. In the gladness of their marital embrace, spouses enact the primeval intention of the Creator, that the "two should become one flesh" (Gen. 2:24, Mk. 10:8). The physical coming together of husband and wife thus fulfills this Scripture passage, and pleases God even as it pleases the lovers.

Within marriage, then, sexual surrender becomes more than just a metaphor for spiritual surrender: sexual surrender becomes an *occasion* for spiritual surrender. Yielding to one another, at once offering and receiving, desiring and desired, husband and wife can make real for one another not only the glory of human love, but the intensity of God's love as well.

As we find in the Song of Songs, "Love is strong as death, passion fierce as the grave. Its flashes are flashes of fire, a raging flame" (Song 8:6).

Twenty centuries ago, Jesus sat with friends and shared good food and drink. Twenty centuries ago, he who is God incarnate walked the fields of Galilee and Judea, watching the birds of the air, and smelling the lilies of the field.

He was called a glutton and a drunkard, but now he is exalted, and for twenty centuries has been worshiped as universal sovereign by men and women who have, unfortunately, not always shared his appreciation of this created realm. For there have been sour-faced Christians in every age. Uptight and unfree, they have given (and give today) a counterwitness to Christ, leading many of those outside the faith to think that loving this Lord leads to diminishment of life and dampening of joy.

Surrender can dispel such gloom, for in surrender we become more and more like the One to whom we give ourselves. Our capacity for pleasure and joy expands as we grow toward that infinite ecstasy which awaits us. Yet even here, even now, our senses may perceive it and our spirits may glimpse its glory. Heaven shines through to earth, and, by God's grace, the surrendered soul will taste it.

FOR YOUR PRAYER

Spending time with our memories of God's goodness is a way of prayer that helps us grow in our ability to appreciate the pleasures and joys of life. After centering yourself in silence, proceed at your own pace.

In the beginning,
    God created the heavens and the earth,
    God made the mountains and streams,
    the fields and the forests, the oceans and lakes,
    the starry skies, the birds and the animals.
When it was finished,
    God saw that creation was good.
You have known the goodness of God's creation.
Remember? *Remember.*
Perhaps you have stood by the sea
    and been deeply cleansed
    by the rhythmic sound of the waves.
Perhaps you have spent time among tall trees
    or savored the serenity that fills the sky at sunset.
Perhaps you have been dazzled
    by the sun glistening upon fresh snow
    or drawn close to a wild animal feeding in a glade
    or quietly watched a lingering bird at your window.
Remember? *Remember.*
Having made so wonderful a home,
    God made wonderful inhabitants.
God made human beings in the divine image,
    male and female God created them,

and saw that they were very, very good.
You have known the goodness of people.
Remember?
Perhaps you have touched an infant's hand in awe,
    or contemplated the mystery in an old person's eyes.
Perhaps you were moved
    by an unexpected act of kindness,
    or transported in the embrace of a spouse.
There are people in your life who have been,
    in their love for you, sacraments of the love of God.
Remember.
Then, in the fullness of time,
    God sent into the world the Word,
    through whom all goodness was made.
God sent Jesus into the world,
    your brother, your savior, your Jesus.
And he was good, and brought good news.
You have known the goodness of Jesus;
    you have heard his good news.
Remember?
Perhaps his presence gave your life new meaning,
    or sustained you in a time of pain or loss.
Perhaps he was the light
    that rescued you from darkness or confusion.
His friendship gives you pleasure, peace, joy, and life.
Remember.
So much God has given, so much God has done. Let your memories move you to gratitude and delight. Ask for the grace to carry them with you as you go from this time of prayer.

CHAPTER 5

SURRENDER IN PRAYER

n the midst of my morning work, the voice of my secretary calls out, "Jim, Monica's here for her appointment." For an hour or so, Monica will get my full attention (or at least, the fullest attention I am able to muster.) The day will include other appointments, phone calls, teaching a class at a local college, and chance encounters of varying length with various people. Then home I go to my wife and four children, a meal, the mail, maybe some games or yard chores. Through it all, my focus of attention must continually change as I move from this to that, from one person to another.

This is life for all of us. From the moment we open our eyes in the morning, we are constantly shifting our attention—from the alarm clock to the stiff muscle, from the temperature of the shower water to the clothes in the closet, from family members at breakfast to getting out the door for work, and so on. Every second we are bombarded with sights, sounds, needs, desires. People move in and out of our circle of awareness, and all the while thoughts and emotions are surfacing within our consciousness. Yet because we are finite creatures, we cannot be fully present to everything that's going on around us and within us: we must be selective.

This is not the case with God, who gives total attention to all things and to each one of us simultaneously. God is so attentive to creation that not one sparrow falls to the ground without God's noticing it; God is so attentive to every human being that "even the hairs of your head are all counted" (Mt 10:30). As the psalmist prayed, "You know when I sit down and when I rise up; you discern my thoughts from far away. You search out my path and my lying down, and are acquainted with all my ways. Even before a word is on my tongue, O Lord, you know it completely" (Ps 139:2–4).

Under the watchful eyes of our Creator, we go about our lives, letting our attention be absorbed by all kinds of things, both worthy and unworthy. Yet there are moments when our attention turns to God. Perhaps we look up from a computer screen to the green of the trees outside our window, and the face of the Divine Lover captures us. Perhaps we are racing between household tasks in preparation for expected company, when an icon on the wall calls us back to our center and evokes a few simple words of praise. Or perhaps we are involved in a religious practice like liturgy, a retreat, or meditation, when we seek to give more sustained attention to the One who made us.

But however and wherever it may happen, when we become consciously present to God, when we shift our attention to God, we are engaging in prayer. We may or may not use words or feel inspired: these conditions are not necessary for prayer to be prayer. It is attention that lies at the heart of prayer, the choice to look toward God that turns any given moment into a moment of prayer.

Have you ever been so involved in a project or activity that you did not notice a friend had stepped into the room? You continue on with your work, unaware of your friend's gaze until something causes you to look up: Surprise! There stands your friend, smiling broadly. It is much like this with prayer.

When we turn our eyes to God we see someone whose eyes are already on us. As Psalm 139 continues:

> Where can I go from your spirit? Or where can I flee from your presence? If I ascend to heaven, you are there; if I make my bed in Sheol, you are there. If I take the wings of the morning and settle at the farthest limits of the sea, even there your hand shall lead me, and your right hand shall hold me fast (Ps 139:7–10).

Early on in the spiritual life, we may find that the practice of giving attention to God in prayer takes effort. God may seem to be at the periphery of our vision, so that shifting our focus to God requires us to move away from what we're focused on at the moment. But as we grow spiritually, this begins to change. God moves more and more into the foreground, not as an object of attention that usurps all others, but as an intensely personal Presence which shines through all else. Little by little, we learn by grace what it means to "pray without ceasing" (1 Th 5:17), to "seek his presence continually" (Ps 105:4).

Whenever we truly give attention to someone, we are yielding to that person, however briefly. To give our attention to anyone is to expose ourselves to that person's influence; we are not easily touched by those we ignore. In like manner, when we consciously turn toward God in prayer we open ourselves and become particularly vulnerable to the power of the Divine Lover.

This can be risky, for the One to whom we give our attention is an almighty, unpredictable, and utterly free Being who will not necessarily act in us according to our expectations. While we know that God loves us passionately and always works for our good, God remains a God of surprises, and the fruit of our prayer will not always be sweetness and serenity. Sometimes we will encounter God as "a sound of sheer silence" (1 Kgs 19:12), and sometimes as "thunder and earthquake and great noise" (Is 29:6). We can never know in advance how our prayer may affect our lives, only that it will.

Of course, all of us at times experience distractions when praying, occasions when our attention to God diminishes or shifts to something else. This is to be expected, and is the result of our finitude and human limitations. When distractions occur, intention can make up for what we lack in attention. Our underlying desire to be fully present with God can carry us through our inability to sustain such presence.

Still, if we find ourselves plagued with distractions, it may be wise to avoid prolonged sessions of prayer in favor of short, frequent prayer. St. Augustine recommended precisely this, in a letter sent to the Roman noblewoman Proba, "so that the alert attention, which is necessary in prayer, does not fade and grow heavy through long, drawn-out periods." Even apart from the question of distractions, carving out a big chunk of time for prayer is next to impossible for many people today, and short, frequent prayer may be a better spiritual goal.

A Capacity for Trust

Authentic prayer is an act of surrender; therefore, it requires trust. Here we need to be especially alert to our own deep capacity for self-deception, for it is entirely possible to go through the motions of prayer without really surrendering. We can use outward forms of prayer and "heap up empty phrases" (Mt 6:7) without actually opening to God and giving God our attention. In fact, we can even use a prayer routine to block out the voice of God. Such prayer without surrender lacks substance; it is not real. Without surrender, religious practice becomes a kind of magic wherein we try to control reality and manipulate God to do our will.

In authentic prayer, we let go and don't try to manage the prayer experience itself. We give our attention to God without determining ahead of time how God will be revealed to us or what God wants to say. When we surrender control of our prayer, the amazing grace of God "is able to accomplish abundantly far more than all we can ask or imagine" (Eph 3:20).

This became real to me in my late twenties, as I faced an important decision. Eager to seek God's guidance, I decided to go on an eight-day directed retreat. Settling down in the chapel on the first day, I began some heavy duty discernment prayer. It wasn't long before I had an overwhelming sense that God was laughing at me—laughing and laughing—and I didn't like it! It was distracting me from my prayer.

This continued throughout the day, and by the time I sat down with my director that evening I was quite annoyed. He listened politely (I wonder now how he ever kept a straight face!), then like a good director he simply said, "Well, Jim, I think you should pay attention to that laughing God."

At dawn the next day, I was in chapel, trying to pray my way to a decision; once again, there was that divine laughter. Remembering my director's advice, I turned from my personal quandary to focus on the God who seemed to mock me. Within minutes, I was transformed. I saw how hilarious I was with my awful solemnity about making a decision, and started laughing, too. God and I laughed through the rest of the retreat, and I never gave another thought to my decision. When I boarded the train to go home at week's end, I found that my decision had already been made within me. I was able to follow it through with peace, and a surprising certainty.

The experience of communal worship offers another opportunity for Christian surrender. When we gather with others for prayer, we turn our eyes toward God through ritual, singing, speaking, and listening. Whether our worship is loud and celebrative or quiet and tranquil, communal surrender is what gives it power and makes it life-giving.

At communal worship, the presider is charged with facilitating the community's focus on the presence of the Divine Lover. But as the power of a river's flow is affected by the number and strength of its tributaries, so the power of a congregation's worship is affected by the prayerfulness of each individual member. We know how the Spirit can move when an assembly of Christians is truly attuned to God. We know, too, the sad lifelessness of the congregation that has lost sight of the One in whose name they are gathered. All the window-dressing in the world cannot make up for that lost focus.

For Catholics, communal worship reaches its zenith in the celebration of the eucharist. Here surrender finds a most perfect expression, for the eucharistic action itself reenacts the total yielding of Jesus to the Father in the sacrifice of Calvary, and renders it sacramentally present for us. As we "approach the throne of grace with boldness" (Heb 4:16) to consume the surrendered body and blood of Jesus, we present ourselves as well to be consumed by Christ. We swallow his body; in turn we are swallowed up in him and made one with all his people. His body in ours, our bodies in his: our continuing choice to belong to God is thus received and ratified at the eucharistic table.

On occasion, people have told me of their concern that receiving the eucharist is not much of a "spiritual experience" for them. Yet no one suggests that it has to be or even that it should be. We do not receive the eucharist in order to attain some kind of religious high: we receive the eucharist as an act of surrender to the Lord Jesus, who instructs us in every age to "Take and eat." He does not say "Take and have a mystical experience"; he does not even say "Take and understand." We are simply to eat and drink, opening ourselves in faith to whatever he may choose to effect in us.

The Darkness of Prayer

As we progress in life along our spiritual journey, sooner or later we pass into periods of darkness when God seems absent. The eye of our attention, accustomed to fixing on his holy presence in prayer, now looks and finds no one there. "I opened to my beloved, but my beloved had turned and was gone....I sought him, but did not find him; I called him, but he gave no answer" (Song 5:6).

Desolate and lonely, we may erroneously attribute this darkness to our own negligence, compounding our misery with feelings of guilt and denigrating self-talk. ("I must have done something wrong." "God must be angry at me." "I wasn't showing enough zeal.") We may throw ourselves into more religious activity, thinking that renewed effort is what is need-ed. We may even find ourselves scrambling back to spiritual practices which once enabled us to taste the divine sweetness, only to find that what "worked" then does so no longer.

But trying to take control and make certain things happen in our prayer will only lead to more frustration, and spiritual exhaustion as well. Clearly, this is not the time for straining after spiritual goals as if the coming of consolation depended on us, for even our ability to pray is itself a gift. When darkness falls, accept the truth that night, too, serves a purpose. Struggling is fruitless: darkness is time for deepening surrender.

In a garden after sunset, it does no good to strain after the lost colors of the flowers, as if we could make them vivid by our insistent staring. We let go of what vision offers by day, and find that other senses arise to replace it. The sweet smells still fill the air, maybe even more so in the soft coolness of evening—or perhaps we just notice them more now that the eyes no longer dominate. We begin to hear the sounds of night creatures—the raspy chirrup of a cricket, the whistling of a frog in a distant pond, a sudden hooting from deep in the woods, or maybe the clear voices of neighbors drifting across the yard. As we relax and yield to the night, even vision is given back to us in a new way. We slowly see shapes and shades of darkness, where once all was opaque. Then comes the glint of a cat's eye, the flash of a firefly, and lo, a sky miraculous with glittering stars.

Something similar happens in the darkness of prayer. Though the whole spiritual landscape seems to have changed, though we may feel we're stumbling around, blind and directionless, deprived of the beauty we had so treasured and loved, we are still standing on firm ground. The One who was there before our night remains utterly present in it. We may not be able to see, but other ways of attending to God are developed in us as we yield to the divine mercy. We may no longer be able to direct our hand to touch, but we can wait expectantly in the darkness to be touched. Waiting expectantly: this becomes our main mode of attention to God.

Suppose you are at home, anticipating a visitor. It is the hour of her planned arrival, and all is ready. You are sitting in your living room, eager for her appearance, poised and alert for any sound, any movement that tells you she's come. You know that she will show up, but nothing you can say or do now will bring her there any sooner. This is the stance of expectant waiting. While in a sense it is passive, it represents a heightened consciousness and a focused awareness: "I wait for the Lord, my soul waits, and in his word I hope; my soul waits for the Lord more than those who watch for the morning" (Ps 130:5–6).

In this spiritual night, we come face to face with our own inability to make God appear on demand. We are stripped of our spiritual self-confidence. We find that we can no longer stand at the front of the temple of our hearts, enumerating for ourselves all our spiritual accomplishments: the ego is powerless and humiliated.

According to St. John of the Cross, the spiritual night is the time we must renew our trust in God "who does not fail those who seek him with a simple and righteous heart; nor does he fail to impart what is needful for the way until getting them to the clear and pure light of love." John continues that we should "allow the soul to remain in rest and quietude" and "care not about thinking and meditating." He goes still further by inviting us to live in darkness "without the concern, without the effort, and without the desire to taste or feel him." Thus we give up all attempts to make the light return.

This is radical surrender, indeed. But as we move toward it, our experience of the darkness changes. Our capacity for God is enlarged by the night; even vision is given back to us in a new way. We see how our gloom is "after all, shade of his hand outstretched caressingly" ("The Hound of Heaven"). We begin to perceive how active God has been during this time when God seemed most absent and inactive, and we know with the utmost certainty that we are the recipients of an unearned, freely given divine love. With John of the Cross, we can exclaim "Ah, the sheer grace!" With him, we can call our experience a "glad night" and a "night more lovely than the dawn!" as we behold anew the sky, miraculous with glittering stars.

How Long?

As any parent with young children will testify, it is a natural human tendency to want to ask, "Are we there yet?" when on a trip. This same question can become an obsession for any one of us on our journey to God. We want to know if we've made spiritual progress, which of the classical stages of spiritual growth we're in, how long it will be before we reach the next turn in the road.

Here, too, God asks for surrender: we are not to trouble ourselves with such questions. Ultimately, all attempts to measure our spirituality will prove useless, and are actually counterproductive. These attempts can become just another form of self-absorption, the very opposite of the contemplative stance we seek to maintain as people of prayer. As an old maxim says, "It's your job to keep your eyes on God, and God's job to keep his eyes on you."

Evelyn Underhill compares the effort to measure our own spiritual growth to the digging up of a flower bulb we have planted. In one of her letters of spiritual direction she writes, "Please at once check the habit of getting the bulb out of the dark to see how it is getting on! It is impossible, and also undesirable for you to judge your own progress. Just go along simply, humbly, naturally, and when tempted to self-occupation of this or any other sort, make a quiet act of trust in God."

Another image, which has been attributed to St. Francis de Sales, compares the spiritual life to an ocean voyage. Early in the journey, you have a clear sense of movement as the port and the shoreline recede in the distance. But once you're at sea there are no longer any easy reference points, no landmarks by which to gauge your speed or direction. How far have you come? How far yet to go? How fast are you moving? These are questions that cannot be answered from your limited perspective. Leave your concerns in the captain's hands. He knows well how to pilot your ship to its intended destination.

Sometimes, what is hidden from our own purview may be clearly manifest to those with whom we share our lives. A good friend, our spouse, or a spiritual director may perceive the workings of grace in us and offer encouragement for the journey. "You are so much more free now than when I first met you." "I've noticed a peace about you lately that wasn't there before." "I remember when an occurrence like that would have left you shaking in your boots. You're more trusting, now." When such affirmation comes our way, we do well to receive it humbly and with gratitude, and give praise to God.

For God can be trusted with attending to our growth. After all, God desires intimacy with us far more than we desire intimacy with God, and knows best how to bring it about. It was out of love and for love that God first "formed my inward parts" and "knit me together in my mother's womb" (Ps 139:13). With fascination and delight, God "beheld my unformed substance" in those months "when I was being made in secret, intricately woven in the depths of the earth." (Ps 139:16,15).

God beholds our every moment, our every heartbeat, our every breath, our every activity, our every encounter. How wonderful that we should be the objects of such constant, affectionate divine regard! What would it mean for us—how would it change our experience of reality—if we could come to a fuller awareness of it? Prayer is the door: surrender is the key.

FOR YOUR PRAYER

I enjoy doing simple awareness exercises with groups involved in learning about Christian prayer. After we participate in a prayer experience such as the one below, discussion follows and participants are asked to share their experience of the exercise. Our conversation becomes more animated when I pose the question "Was what we just did prayer? If you think so, why? If not, what do you think would make it prayer?" Such reflection on what constitutes prayer is always enlightening for all.

Here's an awareness exercise involving a number of senses. Read through it carefully, then give it a try. Notice what it's like for you to be shifting attention, now here, now there.

Take some time to still yourself. Close your eyes, and let go of any worries or concerns, let go of the busyness of the day, and the tumult of thoughts and feelings.

With your eyes still closed, become aware of any sounds that you hear coming to your ears—sounds from nearby, and sounds from far away. Focus your attention on listening to the sounds. Don't try to identify them or think about them…just listen.

Now become aware of physical sensations you might be experiencing in your body. Begin with the top of your head, then move downward to sensations in your feet. Sequentially shift your attention from one part of your body to the next…just feel the sensations.

Open your eyes, and see what is directly before you. Give attention particularly to the elements of shape and color that are there before your eyes…just see.

Conclude by resting in an awareness of God's attentive presence with you. Seek to be open to the Love that God is pouring into you through all your senses.

You may wish to articulate your surrender to God in words. Use your own, or perhaps the beautiful prayer of surrender composed by St. Ignatius that follows:

> *Take, Lord, and receive all my liberty,*
>   *my memory, my understanding,*
>   *and my entire will*
>   *all that I have and possess.*
> *You have given it all to me.*
> *To You, Lord, I return it.*
> *Everything is yours;*
>   *dispose of it according to your will.*
> *Give me only your love and your grace.*
> *That is enough for me.*

CHAPTER 6

RESISTANCE TO SURRENDER

The child was intent and would not be dissuaded. "Want! Want!" he insisted, earnestly stretching his toddler's hand toward the sharp object held behind his father's back. "Want! Want!" he wailed, before crumbling melodramatically into a heap on the ground. There he quivered, and continued whimpering through his tears: "Want! Want! Want!"

All of us are creatures of desire, and we live wanting from the very start. Our early, simple desires for milk and touch and comfort quickly expand to more diverse hungers as we begin to want not just the basics of survival, but certain toys and specific clothes, sharp objects we cannot have, the attention of family and friends—and always, our own way! With maturity comes the driving desire for sexual fulfillment, and a conscious longing for a sense of worth and accomplishment. We may find ourselves wanting status or power, more or different possessions. Some of our desires move us toward goodness and growth and love; some of our desires may tear us from such fruitful ends. What we desire and which desires we choose to act on are obviously questions of great significance.

But in each of us, underneath these manifold human cravings, resides a spiritual longing, a hunger for God—an empty place that can only be filled by the One for whom we've been made. God, after all, was our beginning; God remains our goal and destiny. Is it any wonder that we are ever incomplete, ever unfulfilled apart from God? Is it any wonder that, as St. Augustine wrote, we find our hearts restless and cannot finally rest until we rest in God?

In each of us, there is a hunger for God, a desire for intimacy with God. This has been the human experience from ancient times to the present, and it is beautifully expressed in many of Israel's psalms:

As a deer longs for flowing streams, so my soul longs for you, O God. My soul thirsts for God, for the living God. When shall I come and behold the face of God? (Ps 42:1–2).

O God, you are my God, I seek you, my soul thirsts for you; my flesh faints for you, as in a dry and weary land where there is no water (Ps 63:1).

Words like these resonate in the hearts of believers, for we have tasted the goodness of God, and know what it's like to find refreshment, peace, and joy in our Creator. We know, too, how this taste moves us to want more and more of God, until in all things and in all persons we seek to meet and love the holy Trinity.

People of no faith have this longing, too, though they inter-pret it differently. They have the same empty place inside, but struggle to fill it by all manner of means because they do not understand the ultimate calling of this place. That is why con-version to Christ is often experienced as a coming home. To find at last what we have deeply wanted all our lives is to find not only God but ourselves, as well.

If we are creatures of desire, it is because we have been made in the image and likeness of a God of desire, a God who wants both our existence as the specific human beings we are, as well as our surrender in love. We pray our psalms of long-ing, and and if we listen we may hear God echoing those sacred words: "As a deer longs for flowing streams, so my soul longs for you, Bill." "My soul thirsts for Susan, for the liv-ing Susan. When shall she come and behold my face?" "Tom, you are my Tom, I seek you, my soul thirsts for you...."

Our God wants us; our God is pursuing us! Indeed, to use imagery from the Song of Songs (Song of Solomon), our God is rushing toward us with the eagerness of a young stag, "leaping upon the mountains, bounding over the hills" (2:8). Our God is standing at the door of our hearts, knocking and filled with hope for admission. "Open to me," God says to each of us, calling us by name. "Open to me...my love" (5:2).

We know well that knocking and that divine voice, do we not? The call has come to us repeatedly, since we were very small. "Open to me...." It may come as a whisper in the dark-ness of night, when we can't sleep and our minds are filled with the cares of life, when we are tossing and turning, fretting over who knows what. "Open to me...."

We may hear its sound like a melody in the quiet of a sum-mer's eve, or relaxing after a happy day spent with friends; we may hear it clearly spoken at eucharist or in our private prayer. Then there are the times when the call comes as a roar, with fists pounding on the door, when we've tried to shut out all but our own voices: "OPEN TO ME," God cries.

Here we confront the great paradox of the spiritual life. We long for God, and maintain that there is nothing we want more than to belong to God, to surrender completely. In turn, God longs for us and is here, saying "Yes, surrender! Open the door! Give yourself over!" When there is such mutual agreement on the goal, why does it take us a lifetime to reach this goal? Why are there so few saints among so many who profess faith? It is not God who is the hesitant one in this relationship: we are the ones who hesitate. Against all our better judgment, we resist the love of our God.

Sometimes we resist simply by not praying, not giving any attention to the Divine Lover. As one woman phrased it: "I know God is there, but I won't let myself look into God's eyes." It's easy to find excuses, multiple reasons for not becoming present to God. It's easy for us to let the days slip by with no time for prayer, even as we profess how much we value prayer and want to pray. Ah, but we have places to go, things to do, people to see...our door stays closed.

Resistance to God, however, is not just manifested in the avoidance of prayer. Even when we do make conscious contact with our Maker we are not always cooperative and responsive. We can be like the child who comes to the table but refuses to eat, or someone who goes out on a date but spends the evening looking out the window. In our prayer, we can be like Martha of the gospel story (Lk 10:38–42); we've let Jesus in the house, but we're not going to get too close to him. He can sit over there while we busy ourselves here. To be sure, this is better than leaving Jesus out in the cold entirely. But it's really only halfhearted praying, if such a thing is possible.

Overcoming Fear

Why do we do this? Why do we thwart our deepest human

longing, and resist surrendering to the One who loves us so
truly? Often, the answer is that four-letter word: fear. Poor
broken creatures that we are, we tend to fear intimacy across
the board, and intimacy with God can be particularly frightening.

On the most basic level, it can be frightening simply because
God is the Almighty. In *The Idea of the Holy*, a now classic study
of religious experience, Rudolph Otto speaks of the almost
primitive religious dread an encounter with the Living God
can engender in us. For to meet God is to meet a Being more
unlike than like us, a Being of awesome, overpowering majesty
on whom we totally depend for existence. We can see an example of this fear in the account of the call of the prophet Isaiah
when he trembles before his vision of the Holy One, exclaim-
ing "Woe is me! I am lost" (Is 6:5). We see it, too, in the experience described by Eliphaz the Temanite in the Book of Job:

> Now a word came stealing to me, my ear received the
> whisper of it. Amid thoughts from visions of the night,
> when deep sleep falls on mortals, dread came upon me,
> and trembling, which made all my bones shake. A spirit
> glided past my face; the hair of my flesh bristled. It stood
> still, but I could not discern its appearance. A form was
> before my eyes; there was silence, then I heard a voice....
> (4:12–16)

This awesome fear is in the story of the call of the first disciples in Luke's gospel, when, overcome with amazement at
the miraculous power of Jesus, Peter falls prostrate before him.
"Go away from me, Lord, for I am a sinful man!" Peter begs
(5:8). Mark's gospel frequently comments on how people
responded to Jesus with fear and astonishment (see, for example, 4:41, 5:33, 6:51). People recognized in Jesus something

more than human, a divine presence that stirred a religious awe.

I occasionally hear echoes of primal, holy dread in accounts of people's prayer experiences. "I had an uncanny sense that God was standing right behind me. It sent chills down my spine." "I knew Jesus was right there, calling me. I must admit, I felt like running away as fast as I could." Such in-the-gut fear is real, though it's generally not something people feel comfortable in acknowledging. Some might even interpret such fear as indicating a lack of faith, or as holding to a faulty understanding of God.

Yet however strong our faith may be, however sophisticated our spiritual outlook, we may know religious dread in our meeting with the divine. Our God is a God of mystery who is always more than and other than our limited understanding can encompass or express. When creature and Creator draw near one another, it's natural for the creature to cry "Holy!" When a human being experiences love from the Supreme Being, it's natural for the human to feel somewhat shocked.

The fear of death can also underlie our resistance to God's advances. Whenever we open to God, we open to the One who is our final destiny, our ultimate end. We cannot be present to God without at the same time being present, at least unconsciously, to the fact of our mortality—and that can be scary.

I remember one man telling me, "I never go to hospitals, funeral homes, or churches. They make me nervous." Churches, like hospitals and funeral homes, are places where we come face to face with the reality that we're not going to be here forever. We don't like to be reminded that "All people are grass, their constancy is like the flower of the field. The grass withers, the flower fades, when the breath of the Lord blows upon it" (Is 40:6–7). Since denial of death cannot last long in the presence of God, it can be tempting to just avoid God completely.

There are other fears in the spiritual life that are like those found in any intimate relationship. For example, when we love and are loved by another, our growing oneness with that person can be threatening to our sense of selfhood. We may fear losing ourselves in the beloved's identity, especially if that identity is more strongly developed than our own.

Fear of intimacy can also center around acceptance and rejection. If we let someone into our lives, if we let this person really get close to us and know who we are, will we be accepted? Could we handle being rejected? Still another concern is increased vulnerability, because in giving our hearts to someone we open ourselves to being hurt. We also become aware of how susceptible the other person is to being hurt by us: he says, "I worry that I'll only cause her heartache." She says, "I'm afraid I'll end up hurting him"—and so they stay apart.

Loss of identity, the possibility of rejection, increasing vulnerability: these fears can block our intimacy with other people, and can cause us to keep God at arm's length, too. Sure, we may be able to argue with ourselves intellectually, citing chapter and verse on how God accepts us, how compassionate God is, and how we most fully find ourselves only in God. But it's not always easy to overcome fears that are almost instinctive in nature.

Sometimes, people are afraid that deepening surrender to God will bring about a change in their comfortable routine. This is a valid fear, because it certainly will. When does growing intimacy with anyone not bring about such change? If we cultivate a friendship or pursue a romance, we have to make adjustments in our lives to make space for the burgeoning relationship.

Opening to God inevitably brings a change for the better, but this does not mean it will come easily. We might be involved in some sinful activity that we don't want to give up, like the woman who engages in shady business deals or the man who likes to sleep around. We may suspect that God will call us to more radical action for justice, to be more publicly outspoken in confronting evil. We may, like the man in Mark 10:17–22, be very attached to material possessions and shrink from the possibility that God will take them from us. Whatever the specifics, often this fear is expressed this way: "I'm afraid of what God will say to me."

Accepting Joy

Another intimacy-related fear operative in most of us is more difficult to understand, but seems to be a frequent source of resistance to surrender. I have seen it in myself, as well as in many of the men and women I have worked with over the years. Here is an example from one man's experience; we'll call him Eric:

I went to pray one day in a wooded area, which for some reason or another struck me as a sacred space, perhaps because the place was so naturally beautiful. The God I met there came to me in the image of the Creator. I spent some time in repeatedly acknowledging to God: "I know you have laid all of this out before me." I seemed to notice and appreciate something different in nature each time I repeated the phrase.

I noticed these things: a tiny chipmunk who approached my foot and then scampered away, a delicate bird hopping from rock to rock, the sounds of various creatures I could not see, the breath of the breeze, and a human voice in the distance. Most of all, I was struck by the tops of two very high trees. One of the branches most caught my attention because it appeared to be dancing. The branch itself seemed to be almost still, but the leaves on it were obviously moving. There was a cloud as a backdrop. I can't explain why I felt God was there in all of this, but somehow I was certain he was.

"I know you have laid all this before me." I continually spoke these words. I could not see or hear God, but definitely felt his presence and was overcome with a sense of awe. I was talking to God, and God was with me and in me! The Creator was moving in creation, and filling my being. I felt like Moses must have felt when he found himself standing on holy ground. I basked for a long time in the presence of God in creation, and the presence of God in me. I was moved to tears.

Then, I asked God for a face. I wanted to know how I would continue to recognize him when he came to me. I asked, "How will I know you? How will you make yourself known to me?" God answered—and I was taken— "In countless ways."

All at once, I began to feel unworthy of the time I had spent with God. I started to rush away from the experience, feeling guilty for taking too much from this wonderful God. I wanted to thank him, but I decided I had probably used up my limit. As I began to pull away, I felt God speaking from within my entire being: "Stay with me." I felt surprised and shocked, and stayed for a while longer, with great gratitude.

Filled with joy, but overanxious to step aside and think about what I had experienced, I did not tell God I loved him as I had planned at the outset of my prayer. Nonetheless, I am changed by this experience.

Eric and I enjoyed talking about this beautiful encounter with God, and all its positive effects. When we looked at what was happening toward the end of it ("I started to rush away...feeling guilty for taking too much...used up my limit...began to pull away...."), he could only say that he had become suddenly afraid because he was experiencing "too much spiritual pleasure." God was wooing him, lavishing affection on him. In the end he ran from it in fear, because it felt too good to be true. Eric felt that he didn't deserve the experience—maybe God had given it to the wrong person!

We might identify an element of religious dread in this experience, but repeatedly Eric underlined that he was frightened by how good the experience was, how pleasurable. Did he fear losing himself in God's mystical embrace? In part, that was true. But mostly, he just couldn't accept that God could love him so much. Didn't God see who he was? Didn't God know that he was not the best of Christians? Like a child who's been sampling the freshly baked cookies, Eric figured he'd better get out of the kitchen before anyone got wise to him.

Objectively, fear may seem a strange response to positive encounters with the Divine Lover. Yet obviously it happens, perhaps because deep down we think so little of ourselves that we can't imagine God would think otherwise, or favor us so richly. We may become suspicious when we hear words of tenderness or approval; to accept as true something "too good to be true" would shake our worldview profoundly. We more readily accept a voice of criticism or judgment as being the voice of God.

Still, as the Word of God insists and the experience of believers through the ages confirms, God finds us beautiful despite our sinfulness. God is in love with us, not in some abstract, insubstantial way, but in reality. It is a love we are meant to experience, and it is manifested in the words God speaks to us and in the deeds God does for us. If in our finitude we cannot process too much of this love at once, that's okay. So great is the divine humility that the Creator waits for the creature, respecting our limitations even as we are stretched to accommodate more and more of God.

On our part, overcoming resistance to surrender begins with an honest recognition that we do resist God even as we profess our desire for God. Once, after a talk I gave on resistance in prayer, a man approached me to say that he couldn't relate to the subject at all. "Maybe that's where other people are spiritually," he said, "but I don't resist God, and I'm sure that I don't ever feel fear of him." While it's possible that the man was in an advanced state of sanctity, I'm more inclined to think he was simply in denial. Just as we are sinners until the day we die, we resist God's love until the day we die—though hopefully, less and less as the years pass.

Uncovering and identifying the specific fears that motivate our resistance is also helpful. Are we, in fact, afraid that surrender will require us to make some changes in the way we're going about our lives? Do we have an ingrained fear of the unseen, as did the woman who told me she seldom prayed because it was all "too spooky"? Observing what goes on in us when we interact with God can make us more aware when fear stirs in us. Difficult as it may be, we can learn much about ourselves if we stay with the fear, feeling it fully in the hope it will name itself. (Named fear is easier to work with than a vague apprehension in the soul.)

Trust is integral to surrender, and has a role in dealing with resistance, too. Whatever the fears that impede our intimacy with God, we can still choose to walk forward, one step at a time. We *can* summon our courage and yield ourselves a bit more to God in spite of our fears—then a bit more, and then a bit more. A child only gradually warms to an unfamiliar visiting aunt, first peeking out from behind a chair, then coming closer and closer, then shaking her hand, then finally climbing in her lap. In the same way, our cumulative experience with God will gradually dissolve the misgivings in our hearts.

Let there be no doubt: desire will overcome resistance, and love will conquer all fear. Though our own desire is weak and our love too wavering to carry us, unaided, beyond the massive walls of self—the desire and love of God have no such shortcomings. In truth, it is this longing in the heart of God that moves us through all obstacles. It is the intensity of the divine desire that strengthens desire in us, and draws us to surrender. We want because we are wanted.

"Open to me..." God says to each of us, calling us by name. "Open to me...my love."

FOR YOUR PRAYER

Here are a variety of Scripture texts that speak of God's love. In each is a blank space for your name. After quieting yourself and turning your attention to God, begin to pray one of these verses by speaking it slowly, softly, aloud if possible, inserting your name in the blank.

Stay with one verse, repeating it, hearing God say the words to you personally. Be aware of how it feels to hear those words. Try to take in the affection that God is giving you! Note any resistance to receiving this love, and ask God to help you move through any resistance.

I have loved you, _____, with an everlasting love, so I am constant in my affection for you. (Jer 31:3)

I am holding you by the right hand, _____. I tell you, "Do not be afraid, I will help you" (Is 41:13).

_____, before I formed you in the womb, I knew you (Jer 1:5).

I have called you by your name, _____, and you are mine (Is 43:1).

Does a woman forget her baby at the breast, or fail to cherish the son of her womb? Yet even if these forget, I will never forget you, _____ (Is 49:15).

As the Father has loved me, so I have loved you, _____ (Jn 15:9).

You are precious in my eyes, _____; you are honored and I love you (Is 43:4).

See, _____, I have branded you on the palms of my hands (Is 49:16).

I am with you, to save you, _____ (Jer 30:11).

You did not choose me, _____, no, I chose you (Jn 15:16).

(These texts are taken from the *Jerusalem Bible.*)

CHAPTER 7

THE FINAL SURRENDER

The miracle begins in a moment of ecstasy. A new human life comes into existence, silent and small. In the weeks that follow, the reality of that new life will become manifest in the woman's body. For nine months, that life will grow and blossom into the fullness of the human form.

The child's movements may be felt in the womb as early as the fourth month, a fluttering presence like butterfly's wings. But those first faint flutters soon become kicks and pushes. Mother swells with pregnancy. Her whole being stretches to sustain her sacred trust. With her husband, she waits and watches, aflame with the fires of creation.

Then, when the time is fulfilled, there is a wondrous coming-forth. Through sweat and blood and water, the baby is born, emerging from the darkness of the womb to draw a first breath. In awe of this epiphany, the parents hold their child. Smitten with love, they gaze on the child, enraptured.

Unseen but all-seeing, Another shares their joy. Another is smitten with unutterable love for the new human person cradled in the parent's arms. Nine months ago, God spoke that child's name, calling forth from nothingness the soul now come to birth. Always intended by the Creator, always intended for this man and woman, the child has entered on a life journey which will be filled with surprises.

Hopefully, this child will grow up to know love and find satisfying work. Perhaps he or she will someday marry and become a parent. Maybe this little child will live to be eighty or ninety or one hundred years old. But one thing can be foretold with absolute certainty: the life journey this child has now begun will one day end in death, as all our lives end.

Each of us has had a definite beginning, and each of us will have a specific end. Billions of people have been born, lived, loved, and died before we ever saw light of day; how many billions more will follow? Centuries of time preceded our appearance on the stage of human history; how many centuries more will come and go after our once-new bodies have disintegrated into dust, and all those around us have likewise passed away?

No one is exempt from this temporality. It overrides every distinction between rich and poor, saint and sinner, the most trumpeted celebrity and the most anonymous soul on earth. Even the Lord Jesus chose to embrace it.

It can be sobering to think about these things; we might be tempted to avoid it completely. Yet we cannot live a surrendered life in denial of death. To be sure, there are people who consider it somehow unhealthy to think about death. But just the opposite is true. It's unhealthy *not* to ponder what is inevitable for each of us. As Scripture says, "it is appointed for mortals to die once" (Heb 9:27). If we choose to ignore this truth, then we're out of touch with reality—and that's hardly a healthy state to be in.

"So teach us to count our days that we may gain a wise heart" (Ps 90:12). The author of this psalm, like many of the great Christian teachers and saints, recognized that reflection on our mortality is a way of wisdom which provides a spiritually sound perspective on all else in life. Thus, Chapter 4 of the Rule of St. Benedict advises keeping death daily before one's eyes.

In his *Spiritual Exercises*, St. Ignatius of Loyola recommends imagining oneself at the point of death when involved in a discernment process: "I will consider, as if I were at the point of death, what procedure and norm I will at that time wish I had used in the manner of making the present election. Then, guiding myself by that norm, I should make my decision on the whole matter."

Looking squarely at the reality of death can actually help us to live more completely and contentedly in the present moment. It can open us to the sheer wonder of just being alive. One twenty-five-year-old woman who was battling cancer astonished her family when she told them that the happiest time in her life was the two-year period since her diagnosis. Despite the pain of surgeries and body-wrenching bouts of chemotherapy, she felt she was living each minute more fully than she ever had before. Her father confessed that he felt the same way, and wondered aloud why it sometimes takes a terrible tragedy to jolt us out of living on a superficial level. Why, indeed?

Another young man asserted that cancer had given him a sharpened vision for the ordinary things around him which he usually didn't see. "I never realized how splendid the old pine trees outside my bedroom window were until I had to face the fact that I might not be here to see them much longer," he said.

When we keep death daily before our eyes, we too can know this enhanced keenness of perception and deepened gratitude for the beauty of God's creation.

Reflection on our mortality will help us put our priorities in order. How easy it is to fritter away our time pursuing goals of no consequence! When we live with the awareness that time is running out, we give our attention to what's really important. We see clearly what matters, and what doesn't matter at all.

The Importance of Love

The human relationships God has given us are of primary importance; more valuable, as the gospels affirm, than worldly wealth and success, more important even than religious worship (see, for example, Lk 16:9 or Mt 5:23). The realization that none of us is guaranteed a tomorrow makes us less likely to go to bed today with our feelings still unspoken. We find ourselves more eager to heal hurt relationships, and more willing to forget about the petty wrongs that have been committed against us. We delight in the smile on the face of our husband or wife, the sincerity in our child's heart, our co-worker's sense of humor—and we are sure to tell them. We come to recognize at last that, just as we've always been told, the supreme joy in life is giving and receiving love.

I was moved to hear how one woman, on her deathbed, struggled to convey this knowledge. She was in her final days, weak and drifting in and out of consciousness. At one point, with great exertion she pulled herself up and tried to speak. Intent on being understood, she tried again and again when family members failed to grasp what she said, until they caught her faint, slowly spoken message: "I have finally realized that love is the most important thing." Having delivered this legacy, she could die in peace.

Love is the most important thing! If the womb and the tomb

mark the borders of our temporality, in love we can touch the
frontier of eternity every day of our lives. Love is the foundation and the essence of reality, as it is the very identity of our
God in whom all reality continues to be.

Before the universe came to be, before a single creature was
made, God existed as love. You and I have been individually,
deliberately, and carefully created in the image of this God;
that is to say, you and I were made in love, by love, and capa-
ble of love. It is our purpose and reason for existing. As
Scripture says, God "chose us in Christ before the foundation
of the world to be holy and blameless before him in love" (Eph
1:4). "Therefore be imitators of God, as beloved children, and
live in love, as Christ loved us and gave himself up for us"
(Eph 5:1–2).

Between birth and death we have countless opportunities
to be imitators of God by giving of ourselves to others in love,
and to find ourselves and life's meaning by loving "in truth
and action" (1 Jn 3:18). When we respond to these opportunities, we make manifest the God in whose image we've been
made, and prove ourselves disciples of Jesus Christ (see Jn
13:35). Every authentic act of love is thus an act of spiritual
surrender. Love opens us to know, here and now, the One who
made us, who sustains us, and who awaits us at life's end.

Relationship with God

Awareness of the inevitability of death helps us set our priorities in order, and when we put first things first our relationship with the Creator must surely head the list. This primary
relationship undergirds our existence, and its precedence is
reflected in the first great commandment: "You shall love the
Lord your God with all your heart, and with all your soul, and
with all your mind, and with all your strength" (Mk 12:29–30).

When we have a healthy relationship with God, death is

robbed of its fearful power. If those without faith view death as the termination of a person or a cessation of life, in faith we know otherwise. For though we now see God only "in a mirror, dimly," and know God "only in part," this imperfect perception nevertheless holds the promise of future fullness (1 Cor 13:12). When death comes, it will not be a leaping into darkness, but a face-to-face meeting with the One who has been with us all along; it will be an infinite expansion of all that we've known life to be.

Though our faith does not rest on the validity of so-called "near death" or "afterlife" experiences, I find that my own faith is affirmed by what I've heard from persons who have been resuscitated. Repeatedly, these people have told me of the overwhelming love they encountered at the outer limit of this life. They speak of the all-embracing, intensely personal presence of God and the risen Jesus.

Their fear of death vanishes, they have a newfound peace and sense of purpose in life, and they speak of an eagerness for the day when they will again be fully with Christ in God. In this they echo St. Paul: "I am hard pressed between the two: my desire is to depart and be with Christ, for that is far better; but to remain in the flesh is more necessary for you. Since I am convinced of this, I know that I will remain and continue with all of you" (Phil 1:23–25).

From the very beginning, we have been made for God. Is it any wonder that, daily and forever, we find our delight in receiving God's love and giving ourselves to God in return? Hour by hour, we move toward the consummation of that relationship and foretaste its glory in our practice of spiritual surrender. In the concrete circumstances of our creaturehood, in times of suffering and sorrow, in pleasure and in joy, in prayer and finally in death, surrender brings us to that perfection which is our eternal destiny.

Death is the final surrender. Like every other creaturely limitation, it is not to be simply endured, as if it were only something that happens to us as passive victims. No, because in dying, we can choose God at last with all our being, we can yield ourselves utterly into the hands of our Maker.

When death comes, God will speak our name with exquisite tenderness and call us forth: "Arise, my love, my fair one, and come away; for now the winter is past, the rain is over and gone" (Song 2:10-11).

Then shall we emerge from this mortal nature as from the womb, into a new and everlasting life. It will be like an awakening from sleep. It will be like the embrace of a lover.

The miracle will begin in a moment of ecstasy....

FOR YOUR PRAYER

This meditation will help you focus on the experience of birth and death. You may choose not to do this exercise in one sitting. That's fine. It's important to proceed leisurely.

To begin, find a comfortable and quiet place for this prayer. Settle in to the presence of God. Invite the divine assistance in this time of prayer.

Let yourself drift back in memory now, to imagine a moment you cannot remember: the moment of your birth into this life. Perhaps you have seen photographs of yourself as an infant. Perhaps you have heard stories of your earthly beginning. What were the circumstances of your coming to be?

Imagine what the room might have been like, in which your mother labored in giving you birth. Who would have been with her at the time? Where is your father? What are your parents feeling as this event unfolds?

See yourself coming forth, drawing a first breath. See the faces of those in the room with you. Let yourself see Jesus there too, filled with joy in welcoming you, loving you.

Now move to a future event: the moment of your death. Construct the scenario in your imagination, as you suppose it could occur. Imagine a place for your death. What will be the circumstances of your passing on?

Who will be with you at the time? What are these people feeling as this event unfolds? See their faces. Watch
as you breathe your last breath. Let yourself see Jesus
there too, filled with joy in welcoming you, loving you.

Dialogue with God about what these meditations
have stirred in you.

For Further Reading

De Caussade, Jean-Pierre. *Abandonment to Divine Providence.* New York, NY: Doubleday, 1975.

Doohan, Leonard. *The Contemporary Challenge of John of the Cross.* Washington, D.C.: ICS Publications, 1995.

Ganss, George E., S.J. *The Spiritual Exercises of St. Ignatius: A Translation and Commentary.* St. Louis, MO: The Institute of Jesuit Sources, 1992.

Kavanaugh, K. and Rodriguez, O., trans. *The Collected Works of St. John of the Cross.* Washington, D.C.: ICS Publications, 1991.

Meyer, Charles R. "God and the Problem of Evil." *Chicago Studies,* August 1995.

Oberg, Delroy, ed. *Daily Readings with a Modern Mystic: Selections from the Writings of Evelyn Underhill.* Mystic, CT: Twenty-Third Publications, 1993.

Tagore, R. *Gitanjali.* Flushing, NY: Asia Book Corp., 1987.

Thompson, Francis. *The Hound of Heaven.* Ridgefield, CT: Morehouse Publishing, 1988.

Williams, Charles, ed. *The Letters of Evelyn Underhill.* Allen, TX: Christian Classics, 1989.

Of Related Interest...

The Emotional Jesus
How to Feel Good About Feelings
James Breig
This book helps Christians better understand their emotions from
the unique perspective of Jesus who also experienced human emotions. This
encourages Christians to draw closer to Jesus and express feelings
and emotions as he did.
ISBN: 0-89622-669-7, 72 pp $7.95 (order M-48)

In God's Presence
Centering Experiences for Circles and Solitudes
William Cleary
Appropriate for use by individuals and groups alike, this book of
psalms, meditations, prayers, and poems will help readers find a
connection with God. Readers will delight in Cleary's lighthearted,
imaginative "prayer-poems" prayed from the perspective of bugs
and animals.   ISBN: 0-89622-608-5, 144 pp, $9.95 (order M-08)

Daily Readings With a Modern Mystic
Selections from the Writings of Evelyn Underhill
Delroy Oberg, Editor
The author has selected the best of Evelyn Underhill's writings on
prayer, spiritual life, and mysticism, and organizes them in one-page
reflections that give the reader insight, inspiration, and consolation.
ISBN: 0-89622-566-6, 192 pp, $9.95 (order W-60)

Prayer When It's Hard to Pray
Martin C. Helldorfer
Helldorfer makes clear the point that people's lives—and, thus, their
prayer lives—are an integration of high and low experiences, of
times of feeling in sync with God and others, and times of feeling
alone and out of touch. He offers ways to weather the storminess
that can enter into anyone's prayer life.
ISBN: 0-89622-602-6, 80 pp, $7.95 (order M-18)

Available at religious bookstores or from:

TWENTY-THIRD PUBLICATIONS
P.O. Box 180 • Mystic, CT 06355

For a complete list of quality books and videos call:
1 - 8 0 0 - 3 2 1 - 0 4 1 1